The LITTLE BLACK DISNEY SONGBOOK

ISBN: 978-1-5400-5659-7

Visit Hal Leonard Online at
www.halleonard.com

Contact us:
Hal Leonard
7777 West Bluemound Road
Milwaukee, WI 53213
Email: info@halleonard.com

In Europe, contact:
Hal Leonard Europe Limited
42 Wigmore Street
Marylebone, London, W1U 2RY
Email: info@halleonardeurope.com

In Australia, contact:
Hal Leonard Australia Pty. Ltd.
4 Lentara Court
Cheltenham, Victoria, 3192 Australia
Email: info@halleonard.com.au

The LITTLE BLACK DISNEY SONGBOOK

**BASED ON THE "WINNIE THE POOH" WORKS, BY A. A. MILNE AND E. H. SHEPARD*

Alice in Wonderland

from ALICE IN WONDERLAND

Words by Bob Hilliard
Music by Sammy Fain

Gdim7 G D7 Am7 F#7 Bm7 E7 A7

Verse 1

```
Gdim7 G   D7 G
Al  - ice in Wonderland.
Am7          D7    G
How do you get to Wonderland?
Am7       D7     G
Over the hill or underland
    Am7   D7       G
Or just be-hind the tree?
```

Verse 2

```
Gdim7 G        D7 G
When clouds go rolling by,
Am7        D7       G
They roll a-way and leave the sky.
Am7            D7       G
Where is the land be-yond the eye
      F#7     Bm7   E7
That people cannot see?
```

Bridge

```
Am7       D7    G
   Where can it be?
Am7    D7 G
Where do  stars go?
Am7            D7       G
Where is the crescent moon?
       F♯7   Bm7  E7
They must be     somewhere
        Am7         D7
In the sunny after-noon.
```

Verse 3

```
Gdim7 G  D7 G
Al   -  ice in  Wonderland.
Am7            D7      G
Where is the path to Wonderland?
Am7       D7     G        A7
Over the hill or here or there?
  Am7  D7  G
I won - der  where.
```

Almost There

from THE PRINCESS AND THE FROG

Music and Lyrics by Randy Newman

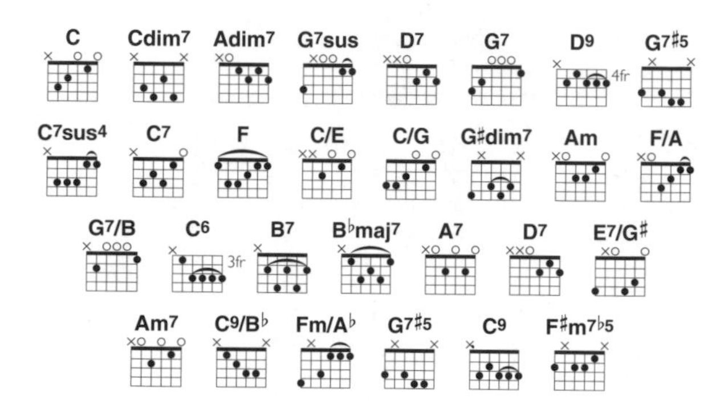

Verse 1

C Cdim7 C
'Mama, I don't have time for dancin'.
Adim7 G7sus4 C
That's just gonna have to wait a while.
Cdim7 C
Ain't got time for messin' around,
D7 G7
And it's not my style.
D9 G7♯5 C7sus4 C7
This old town can slow you down,
F C/E D7
People takin' the easy way,
C/G G♯dim7 Am
But I know ex-act-ly where I'm goin'.
D7 G7
I'm gettin' closer and closer ev'ry day.

Chorus 1

C6 B7 B♭maj7 A7
And I'm al - most there,
F C/E D7
I'm al - most there.
C/G E7/G♯ Am7
People down here think I'm crazy,
D7 G7
But I don't care.
C6 B7 B♭maj7 A7
Trials and tri-bu-la-tions,
F C/E D7
I've had my share.
C/G E7/G♯ Am7
There ain't nothing gonna stop me now
D7 G7sus4 C C9/B♭ F/A Fm/A♭ C/G G7♯5
'Cause I'm al - most there.

Verse 2

C Cdim7 C
I re-mem-ber Daddy told me
F C/E D7
Fairy tales can come true,
C/G E7/G♯ Am7
But you gotta make 'em happen;
D7 G7
It all depends on you.
C G7♯5 C9
So I work real hard each and ev'ry day.
F C/E D7 C/G
Now things for sure are going my way.
E7/G♯ Am7
Just doing what I do,
D7 G7
Look out, boys, I'm comin' through.

Chorus 2

```
                C6  B7          B♭maj7 A7
And I'm al - most there,
F         C/E          D7
   I'm al - most there.
C/G             E7/G#               Am7
People gonna come here from ev'rywhere,
                D7  G7sus4   C
And I'm al - most there,
       D7  G7sus4   C  C9/B♭  F/A  Fm/A♭
I'm al - most there.
```

Interlude

```
| C     C9/B♭     | F/A     Fm/A♭  |

| C   C9/B♭  | F/A  Fm/A♭  | G7#5    |
```

Bridge

```
F#m7♭5        G7#5            C9
There's been trials and tri-bu-la-tions.
F                       C/E      D7
   You know I've had my share.
             C/G              E7/G#
But I've climbed a moun  -  tain,
     Am7
I've crossed a river,
                D7  G7sus4    C
And I'm al - most there.
A7     D7  G7        C
  I'm al - most there.
A7     D9  G7sus4  C      C9/B♭
  I'm al - most      there.
```

Outro

```
| F/A   Fm/A♭  | C/G   C/E    | D7    G7    |

| C  C9/B♭ | F/A Fm/A♭ | C/G  N.C. |   G7 C  |
```

The Aristocats

from THE ARISTOCATS

Words and Music by Richard M. Sherman and Robert B. Sherman

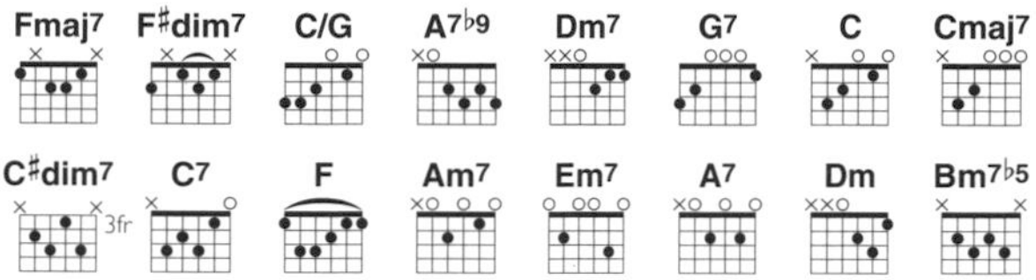

Fmaj7 F♯dim7 C/G A7♭9 Dm7 G7 C Cmaj7

C♯dim7 (3fr) C7 F Am7 Em7 A7 Dm Bm7♭5

Intro | Fmaj7 F♯dim7 | C/G A7♭9 |

| Dm7 G7 | C |

Verse 1

```
C                  Cmaj7
Which pet's ad-dress
         C♯dim7 Dm7    G7
Is the finest   in   Par-is?
Dm7               G7
Which pets pos-sess
      Dm7    G7    C
The longest ped-i-gree?
              Cmaj7
Which pets get
    C7              F
To sleep on velvet mats?
       F♯dim7    C/G    A7♭9   Dm7  G7  C
Na - tur-elle - ment! The a-ris  -  to - cats!
```

Verse 2

C   Cmaj7
Which pets are blessed
**   C♯dim7 Dm7   G7**
With the fairest forms and faces?
Dm7   G7
Which pets know best
**   Dm7   G7   C**
All the gentle social graces?
**   Cmaj7**
Which pets live
**   C7   F**
On cream and loving pats?
**   F♯dim7   C/G   A7♭9 Dm7 G7 C**
Na - tur-elle - ment! The a-ris - to - cats!

Bridge 1

N.C.   Dm7   G7   Dm7
They show a-ris-to-ca-tic bearing
G7   C
When they're seen
**   Am7**
Upon an airing,
**   Dm7   G7   Dm7**
And a-ris-to-ca-tic flair
** G7   C**
In what they do
**   Cmaj7**
And what they say!
** Em7 A7   Em7   A7**
A-ris-to-cats are never found
** Dm   Bm7♭5**
In alleyways or hanging 'round
**   A7**
The garbage cans where
**   Dm7   G7**
Common kitties play.

```
            C                  Cmaj7
Verse 3     Which pets are known
                     C#dim7      Dm7      G7
            To never show their claws?
            Dm7                 G7
            Which pets are prone
               Dm7    G7  C
            To hardly any flaws?
                      Cmaj7
            To which pets
                   C7                    F
            Do the others tip their hats?
                F#dim7  C/G     A7b9   Dm7   G7   C
            Na-tur-elle-ment! The a-ris  -  to - cats!
```

```
Instru      ||: C        | Cmaj7     |   C#dim7 | Dm7  G7 |

            |            |           | Dm7  G7  | C       |

            | C          | Cmaj7     | C7       | F       |

            | F  F#dim7 | C/G  A7b9 | Dm7  G7  | C      :||
```

Bridge 2 — *As Bridge 1*

Verse 4 — *As Verse 3*

```
            F   F#dim7  C/G
Outro       Na-tur-elle-ment!
            F   F#dim7  C/G
            Na-tur-elle-ment!
            F   F#dim7  C/G
            Na-tur-elle-ment!
            A7b9   Dm7  G7  C
            The a-ris  -  to - cats!
```

Arabian Nights

from ALADDIN

Music by Alan Menken
Lyrics by Howard Ashman

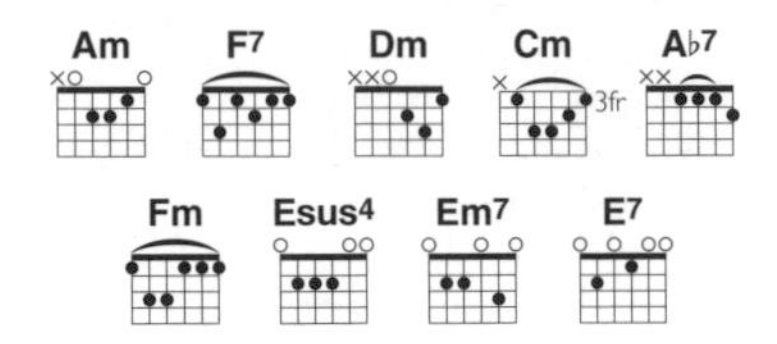

Intro | **Am** | **Am** | **Am** | **Am** |

Verse 1

```
     Am                         F7
Oh, I come from a land, from a faraway place
           Dm              Am
Where the caravan camels roam.
           Cm                            A♭7
Where it's flat and immense and the heat is intense.
        Fm                 Am
It's bar-ba-ric, but hey, it's home.
          F7                              Am
When the wind's from the east and the sun's from the west,
        F7                Esus4
And the sand in the glass is right,
         Am                       F7
Come on down, stop on by, hop a carpet and fly
      Esus4        Am
To an-oth-er  Arabian night!
```

Chorus 1

```
N.C.          Am      Cm
     Arabian nights,
              Am
Like Arabian days
Cm                    Am      Em7        Am
     More often than not are hotter than hot
     F7          E7
In a lotta good ways.
N.C.        Am      Cm
    Arabian nights
                 Am
'Neath Arabian moons
Cm                Am             Em7         Am
    A fool off his guard could fall and fall hard
     F7        E7     Am
Out there on    the dunes.
```

The Ballad of Davy Crockett

from DAVY CROCKETT

Words by Tom Blackburn
Music by George Bruns

Verse 1

```
E                                  A            E
Born on a mountaintop in Tennessee,
                            F♯             B7
Greenest state in the land of the free.
E                                    A              F♯m
Raised in the woods so's he knew ev'ry tree,
B7                                        E
Kilt him a b'ar when he was only three.
```

Chorus 1

```
E       A       E
Davy, Davy Crockett,
B7                       E
King of the wild fron-tier!
```

Verse 2

```
E                                           A             E
Fought single-handed through the Injun war,
                                         F♯               B7
Till the Creeks was whipped an' peace was in store
     E                                 A              F♯m
An' while he was handin' this risky chore,
B7                                  E
Made himself a legend for evermore.
```

Chorus 2

```
E       A       E
Davy, Davy Crockett,
     B7                     E
The man who don't know fear!
```

The Bare Necessities

from THE JUNGLE BOOK

Words and Music by Terry Gilkyson

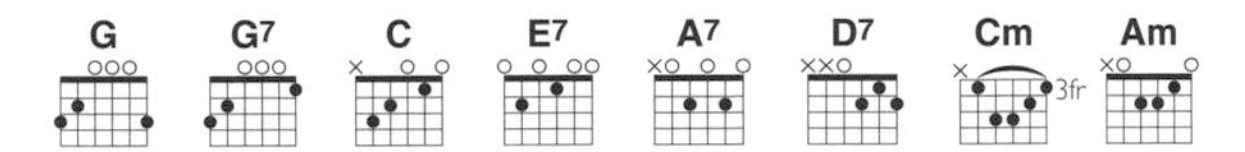

To match original recording, place capo on 5th fret

Verse

N.C. G G7
Look for the bare ne-ces-si-ties,
C
The simple bare necessities,
G7 E7 A7
For-get about your worries and your strife.
D7 G G7
I mean the bare ne-ces-si-ties
C
Or Mother Nature's recipes
G E7 A7 D7 G
That bring the bare ne-ces-si-ties of life.
D7 G
Wherever I wander, wherever I roam,
D7 G G7
I couldn't be fonder of my big home.
C Cm
The bees are buzzin' in the tree
G A7
To make some honey just for me,
Am C D7 G
The bare ne-ces-si-ties of life will come to you.

Be Our Guest

from BEAUTY AND THE BEAST

Music by Alan Menken
Lyrics by Howard Ashman

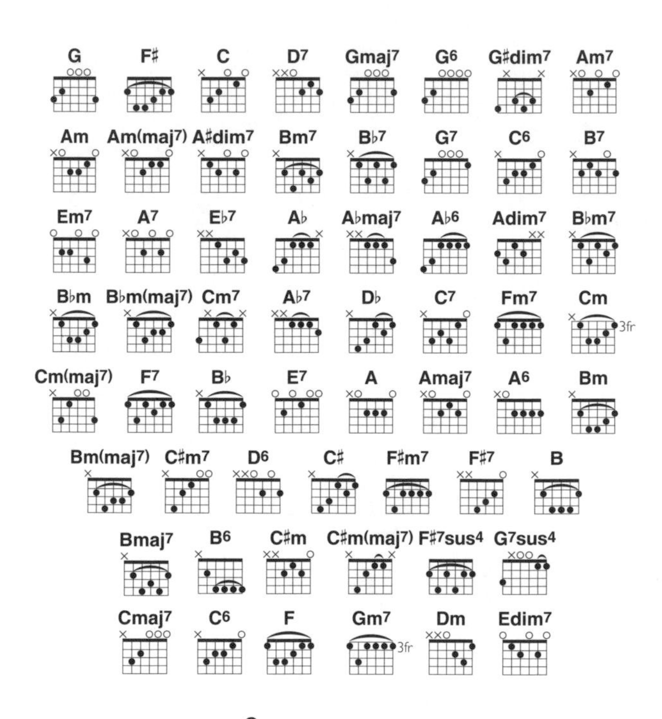

Intro

G
Lumiere: Ma chere Mademoiselle,

F♯
It is with deepest pride and greatest pleasure

C
That we welcome you tonight.

And now, we invite you to relax.

D7
Let us pull up a chair as the dining room proudly presents

your dinner!

Verse 1

```
         G               Gmaj7
Be our guest! Be our guest!
          G6              G
Put our service to the test.
                                    G♯dim7
Tie your napkin 'round your neck, cherie,
      Am7                D7
And we'll provide the rest.
           Am                Am(maj7)
Soup du-jour! Hot hors d'oeuvres!
           Am7        D7
Why, we only live to serve.
         Am7                 A♯dim7
Try the grey stuff. It's de-li-cious!
           Bm7        B♭7       Am7
Don't be-lieve me? Ask the dishes!
D7         G                 Gmaj7
They can sing! They can dance!
          G6
After all,   Miss, this is France!
G                            G7            C
   And a dinner here is never second best.
N.C.        B7
Go on, un-fold your menu.
        Em7          A7                 Am7
Take a glance and then you'll be our guest,
           D7     G       E♭7
Oui, our guest. Be our guest!
```

Verse 2

A♭ A♭maj7
Beef ra-gout! Cheese souf-flé!
A♭6 A♭
Pie and pudding "*en flam-bé!*"
Adim7 B♭m7 E♭7
We'll prepare and serve with flair a cu-li-na-ry ca-ba-ret.
B♭m B♭m(maj7)
You're a-lone and you're scared,
B♭m7 E♭7
But the banquet's all pre-pared.
B♭m7 G♯dim7
No one's gloomy or com-plaining
Cm7 B7 B♭m7
While the flatware's enter-taining.
E♭7 A♭ A♭maj7 A♭6 A♭
We tell jokes. I do tricks with my fellow can-dle-sticks.
A♭maj7 A♭7 D♭
Mugs: And it's all in perfect taste. That you can bet!
N.C. C7
All: Come on and lift your glass.
Fm7 B♭7 B♭m7
You've won your own free pass to be our guest.
E♭7 Cm Cm(maj7) F7
Lumiere: If you're stressed it's fine dining we sug-gest.
B♭m7 Fm7 E♭7 A♭ C
All: Be our guest! Be our guest! Be our guest!

Bridge

Fm7 C
Lumiere: Life is so unnerving for a servant who's not serving.
Adim7 B♭
He's not whole without a soul to wait up-on.
A♯dim7 Fm7
Ah, those good old days when we were useful.
B♭m7 C7
Suddenly, those good old days are gone.
Fm7
Ten years we've been rusting,
C
Needing so much more than dusting.
Adim7 B♭
Needing exercise, a chance to use our skills.
A♯dim7 Fm7
Most days we just lay around the castle.
B♭m7 E♭7
Flabby fat and lazy. You walked in, *and oopsadaisy!*

```
            E7   A            Amaj7
*Verse 3*   It's a guest! It's a guest!
                 A6               A
            Sakes a-live, well, I'll be blessed.
                                              A#dim7
            Wine's been poured, and thank the Lord,
                       Bm7            E7
            I've had the napkins freshly pressed.
                    Bm                Bm(maj7)
            With des-sert she'll want tea.
                    Bm7                 E7
            And, my dear, that's fine with me.
                     Bm7                Adim7
            While the cups do their soft-shoeing
                   C#m7      C7     Bm7       E7
            I'll be bubbling! I'll be brewing!
                   A              Amaj7
            I'll get warm, piping hot.
                   A6               A
            Heaven sakes! Is that a spot? Clean it up...
               Amaj7    A7           D
            We want the company im-pressed!
            N.C.        C#7
            We've got a lot to do.
                           F#m7    B7                Bm
               Is  it one lump or two for you, our guest?
                            E7
            All: She's our guest!
                                       C#m7           F#7
            Mrs. Potts: She's our guest! She's our guest!
```

Verse 4

B Bmaj7
Be our guest! Be our guest!
B6 B
Our com-mand is your re-quest.
Adim7 C♯m
It's ten years since we had anybody here,
F♯7
And we're ob-sessed!
C♯m C♯m(maj7)
With your meal, with your ease,
C♯m7 F♯7
Yes, in-deed, we aim to please.
F♯7sus4 F♯7 G7sus4
While the candlelight's still glowing, let us help you,
G7 C Cmaj7
We'll keep going course by course, one by one!
C6 C/G
'Til you shout, "*Enough, I'm done!*"
Cmaj7 C7 F
Then we'll sing you off to sleep as you di-gest.
E7
Tonight you'll prop your feet up!
Am7 D7
But for now, let's eat up!
Dm Edim7 Dm
Be our guest! Be our guest! Be our guest!
G7sus4 G7 C
Please, be our guest!

Bella Notte

from LADY AND THE TRAMP

Music and Lyrics by Peggy Lee and Sonny Burke

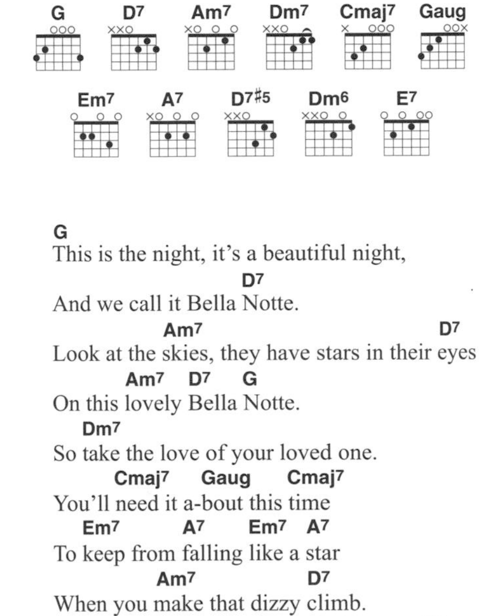

Verse

```
G
This is the night, it's a beautiful night,
                              D7
And we call it Bella Notte.
                 Am7                              D7
Look at the skies, they have stars in their eyes
           Am7    D7    G
On this lovely Bella Notte.
    Dm7
So take the love of your loved one.
         Cmaj7    Gaug    Cmaj7
You'll need it a-bout this time
    Em7          A7       Em7   A7
To keep from falling like a star
                Am7            D7
When you make that dizzy climb.
D7♯5    G                    Dm6          E7
For     this is the night and heavens are right
           Am7    D7    G
On this lovely Bella Notte.
```

Beauty and the Beast

from BEAUTY AND THE BEAST

Music by Alan Menken
Lyrics by Howard Ashman

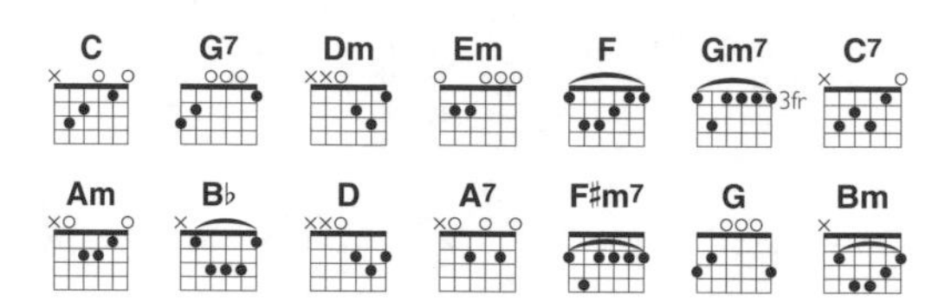

To match original recording, place capo on 1st fret

Verse 1

C G7 C Dm
Tale as old as time, true as it can be.
C Em
Barely even friends,
F G7
then somebody bends un-ex-pec-ted-ly.
C G7 C Gm7
Just a little change. Small, to say the least.
C7 F Em Dm
Both a little scared, neither one pre-pared.
G7 C G7
Beauty and the Beast.

Bridge

G7 Em F Em
Ever just the same, ever a sur-prise.
F Em Am B♭ C
Ever as be-fore, ever just as sure as the sun will rise.

```
            D                  A7   D                    A7
Verse 2       Tale as old as time,    tune as old as song.
            D                   F#m7                        G
              Bittersweet and strange, finding you can change,
                               A7
            Learning you were wrong.
            D                  A7  D                 Am
              Certain as the sun    rising in the East,
            D               G                      Em
            Tale as old as time, song as old as rhyme.
            A7                D
            Beauty and the Beast.
            Bm                 G                      Em
              Tale as old as time, song as old as rhyme.
            A7                D
            Beauty and the Beast.
```

Belle

from BEAUTY AND THE BEAST

Music by Alan Menken
Lyrics by Howard Ashman

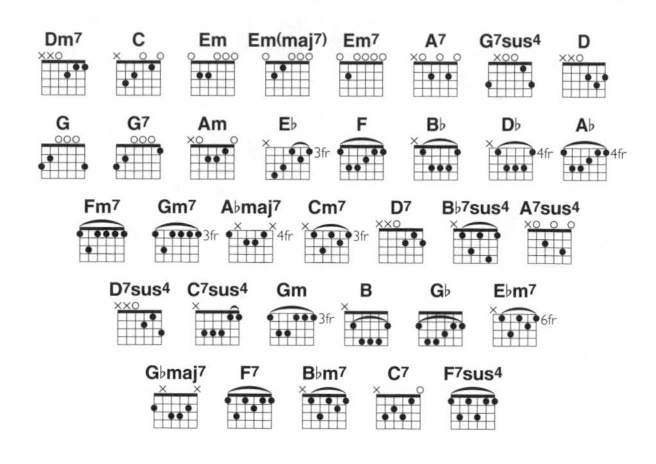

Intro

```
        Dm7                      C
Little town, it's a quiet village.
        Dm7                        C
Ev'ry day like the one be-fore.
        Em      Em(maj7) Em7    A7
Little town, full   of   little  people
          G7sus4
Waking up to say
C
Bonjour!
D   C
    Bonjour!
D   G
    Bonjour!

Bonjour!

Bonjour!
```

Verse 1

```
C                                G7       C
   There goes the baker with his tray, like always,
Am                                  G       C
   The same old bread and rolls to sell.
      E♭         F        B♭
Ev'ry morning just the same
          D♭          E♭        A♭
Since the morning that we came
        Fm7       Gm7      A♭maj7
To this poor pro-vin-cial town.
      G7          C
Good morning, Belle.
```

Interlude 1

```
C
Morning, Monsieur
                            G7sus4  G7
Where are you off to?

The bookshop.
C
I just finished the most wonderful story
        G7sus4                     G7
about a beanstalk and an ogre and a...
C
Oh, that's nice. Marie!

The baguettes!

Hurry up!
```

Verse 2

```
C                                      G7     C
   Look, there she goes. That girl is strange, no question.
Am                                  G           C
   Dazed and dis-trac-ted, can't you tell?
        E♭       F    B♭
Never part of any crowd,
              D♭           E♭          A♭
'Cause her head's up on some cloud.
              Fm7  Gm7      A♭maj7  G7        C
No deny-ing, she's a funny  girl, that Belle.
```

Bridge 1

F
Bonjour!

Good day!

C
How is your fam'ly?

F
Bonjour!

Good day!

C
How is your wife?

A♭
I need six eggs.

E♭
That's too expensive.

Cm7 D7 G7sus4 G C
There must be more than this pro-vin-cial life

Interlude 2

C
Ah, Belle

G7sus4 G
Good morning, I've come to return the book I borrowed.

C
Finished already?

G7sus4 G
Oh, I couldn't put it down! Have you got anything new?

C G7sus4 G
Not since yesterday!

C G7sus4 G
That's alright, I'll borrow... this one.

E♭
That one? But you've read it, twice!

B♭7sus4
Well it's my favorite,

B♭ E♭
Far-off places, daring sword fights,

B♭7sus4 B♭
Magic spells, a prince in disguise...

C G7sus4
If you like it all that much, it's yours.

G
But, Sir!

C
I insist!

G7sus4 G
Well, thank you! Thank you very much!

```
            C                                      G7    C
Verse 3       Look, there she goes. The girl is so peculiar.
            Am                  G        C
              I wonder if she's feeling well.
                     E♭        F       B♭
            With a dreamy, far off look
                     D♭              E♭  A♭
            And her nose stuck in a book,
                     Fm7    Gm7   A♭maj7
            What a puzzle to the rest of us is Belle.

            F          G7sus4    Em
Bridge 2    Oh, isn't this     a-maz-ing!
            A7sus4    A7       D7sus4         G7sus4 C7sus4  C  C7sus4  C
              It's my fav'rite part because you'll  see.
            F  C  Dm7              G7               Em7
            Here's      where she meets Prince Charming,
            A7sus4     A7          D7sus4           D7
              But she won't dis-co-ver that it's him
                                 E♭      Dm7      G
                   'til chapter three.
```

```
              C                                G7      C
Verse 4            Now it's no wonder that her name means 'Beauty.'
              Am                                G    C
                 Her looks have got no pa-ra-llel.
                    E♭          F          B♭             D♭            E♭       A♭
              But be-hind that fair fa-çade I'm a-fraid she's rather odd.
                   Fm7       G7          A♭maj7 Gm7
              Very diff'rent from the rest  of  us.
                     Fm7      G7        A♭maj7 Gm7
              She's nothing like the rest  of  us.
                  Fm7        Gm7        A♭maj7  G7   C
              Yes, diff'rent from the rest  of  us is Belle.
```

```
              C
Interlude 3   Woah, you didn't miss a shot, Gaston!
              G7sus4                    G
              You're the greatest hunter in the whole world!
              E♭
              I know.

                         B♭7sus4                      B♭
              No beast alive stands a chance against you,
              E♭
              And no girl for that matter...
                 B♭7sus4               B♭               C
              It's true, LeFou, and I've got my sight set on that one
              G7sus4                    G
              The inventor's daughter?
                           C                            G7sus4
              She's the one, the lucky girl I'm going to marry.
              G
              But she's...
                             B♭
              The most beautiful girl in town.

              I know, but...
                                            F             B♭
              That makes her the best. And don't I deserve the best?
                                                      F
              But of course! I mean, you do, but I...
```

```
               B♭
Verse 5        Right from the moment when I met her, saw her,
               Gm                           F      B♭
                  I said she's gorgeous, and I fell.
                        D♭              E♭    A♭
               Here in town there's only she
                       B        D♭     G♭
               Who is beau-ti-ful as me,
                       E♭m7   Fm7     G♭maj7  F7     B♭
               So I'm making plans to woo and marry Belle.

               E♭
Bridge 3          Look, there he goes!
                        B♭
               Isn't he dreamy?
               E♭                                 B♭
                  Monsieur Gaston, oh, he's so cute.
               G♭
                  Be still, my heart!
                            D♭
               I'm hardly breathing.
                     B♭m7  C7       F7sus4     F7
               He's such a tall, dark, strong and handsome brute.
```

Bridge 4

```
C
  Bonjour! Pardon!

Good day! Mais oui!
               G
You call this bacon?
C
  What lovely flow'rs!

Some cheese:

Ten yards! One pound. 'Scuse me.
             G
I'll get the knife.
               E♭
Please let me through.

This bread,

Those fish, it's stale. they smell.
                B♭
Madame's mis-tak-en.

  Well, maybe so.
     Gm7    A7                 D7sus4 D7
There must be more than this pro-vin-cial life.
G7sus4 G7
Just   watch!

I'm going to make Belle my wife.
```

Verse 6

```
C
Look, there she goes!
    G7  C
That girl is strange but special,
Am                 G        C
  A most peculiar Mad'moi-selle.
     F  G    C       E♭    F      B♭
It's a pity and a sin: she doesn't quite fit in,
             Gm7  Am7 B♭    Am7
'Cause she really is a  funny girl.
  Gm7    Am7 B♭     Am7
A beauty, but a funny girl.
    Gm7   Am7 B♭      A7sus4  A  D
She really is a  funny girl,   that Belle!
```

Bibbidi-Bobbidi-Boo

(The Magic Song)

from CINDERELLA

Words by Jerry Livingston
Music by Mack David and Al Hoffman

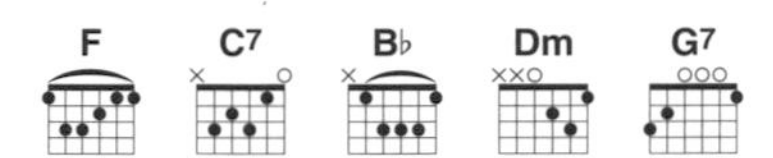

To match original recording, place capo on 3rd fret

```
              F
*Verse 1*     Salagadoola, menchicka boola, bibbidi-bobbidi-boo.
              C7
              Put 'em together and what have you got?
                                F
              Bibbidi-bobbidi-boo.

              F
*Verse 2*     Salagadoola, menchicka boola, bibbidi-bobbidi-boo.
              C7
              It'll do magic believe it or not,
                                F
              Bibbidi-bobbidi-boo.

              B♭                    F           Dm
*Bridge*      Salagadoola means menchicka booleroo,
                       G7                                 C7
              But the thingamabob that does the job is bibbidi-bobbidi-boo.

              F
*Outro*       Salagadoola, menchicka boola, bibbidi-bobbidi-boo.
              C7
              Put 'em together and what have you got?
                                                                  F
              Bibbidi-bobbidi, bibbidi-bobbidi, bibbidi-bobbidi-boo.
```

Breaking Free

from HIGH SCHOOL MUSICAL

Words and Music by Jamie Houston

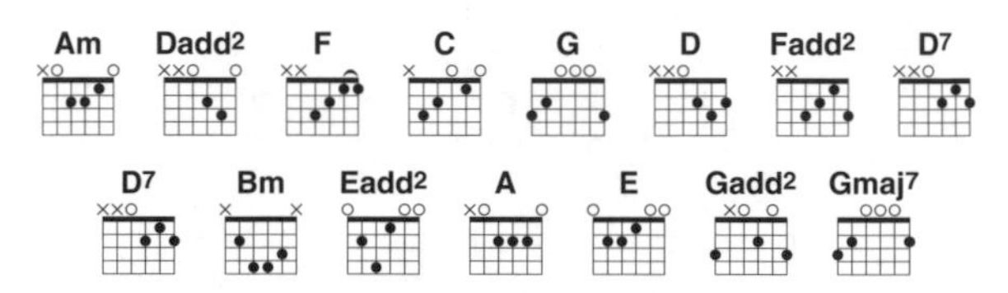

To match original recording, place capo on 3rd fret

```
               Am
Intro          We're soarin',
               Dadd2
               Flyin'.
               F                         C              G              Am
               There's not a star in hea - ven that we   can't reach.
                              D
               If we're try  -  in',
                          Fadd2
               So we're breakin' free.

               Am                                D
Verse 1          You know the world can see   us
               F                   C                   G            Am
                 In a way that's dif - f'rent from who   we are
                                    D
               Creating space be-tween us,
                    F                    C     G
               Till we're seperate hearts.
               F
               But your faith,
                         D7
               It gives    me strength
               Fadd2
               Strength to believe
```

Chorus 1

Am
We're soarin',
D
Flyin'.
F C G Am
There's not a star in hea - ven that we can't reach.
D
If we're try - in',
Fadd2
Yeah, we're breakin' free.

Oh, we're breakin' free.

Verse 2

Am D
Can you feel it build - ing,
F C G Am
Like a wave the o - cean just can't con-trol
D F C G
Connected by a feel - in', oh, in our very souls,
F D7
Rising till it lifts us up
Fadd2
So everyone can see?

Chorus 2 *As Chorus 1*

```
              Am
*Chorus 3*    Runnin',
                     D
              Climb - in',
                 F
              To get to that place
                    C            G        Am
              To be   all that we   can be.
                         D
              Now's the time,
                        Fadd2
              So we're breakin' free.
                     C             G
              We're breakin' free.

              F
*Bridge*        More than hope, more than
              D7
                Faith, this is truth, this is fate;
              F
                And together, we see it comin'.

              More than you, more than me,
              D7
                Not a want, but a need:
              F
                Both of us breakin' free.
```

```
           Bm
*Chorus*   Soarin',
           Eadd2
           Flyin'.
           G                         D            A            Bm
           There's not a star in hea - ven that we  can't reach.
                       E
           If we're try - in',
                        G
           Yeah, we're breakin' free.
                  Bm
           We're runnin',
                       E
           Ooh, climb  -  in'
              G                         D            A        Bm
           To get to the place to be  all that we  can be.
                            E
           Now's the time,
                      Gadd2
           So we're breakin' free.

           Oh, we're breakin' free.

           Bm                             E
*Outro*      You know the world can see  us
           Gadd2           D                         A      Gmaj7
             In a way that's diff'rent from who  we are.
```

Can You Feel the Love Tonight

from THE LION KING

Music by Elton John
Lyrics by Tim Rice

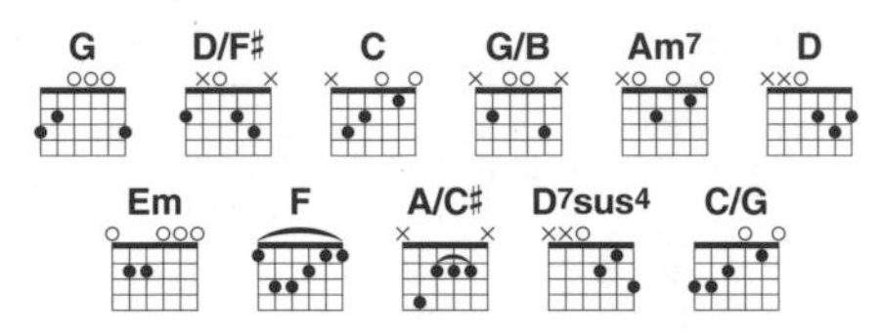

To match original recording, place capo on 3rd fret

Intro | G D/F♯ | C G | C G/B | D/F♯ G Am7 G/B |

Verse 1

C G/B C G/B
There's a calm sur-ren-der to the rush of day,
C G/B Am7 D
When the heat of a rolling wind can be turned a-way.
C G/B C G/B
An enchanted moment, and it sees me through.
C Em F D
It's enough for this restless warrior just to be with you.

Chorus 1

G D/F♯ Em C
And can you feel the love to-night?
G C A/C♯ D
It is where we are.
C G/B Em C
It's enough for this wide-eyed wanderer
Am7 G/B C A/C♯ D
That we got this far.
G D/F♯ Em C
And can you feel the love to-night,
G C A/C♯ D
How it's laid to rest?
C G/B Em C
It's enough to make kings and vagabonds
Am7 G/B C D7sus4 C/G G
Be-lieve the very best.

Interlude *As Intro*

Verse 2

C   G/B   C   G/B
There's a time for ev'ryone if they only learn
C   G/B   Am7   D
That the twisting ka-lei-do-scope moves us all in turn.
C   G/B   C   G/B
There's a rhyme and reason to the wild out-doors
C   Em
When the heart of this star-crossed voyager
F   D
Beats in time with yours.

Chorus 2 *As Chorus 1*

Outro

C   G/B   Em   C
   It's enough   to make kings and vagabonds
     Am7   G/B C   D7sus4 C/G G
Be-lieve   the   very best.

Chim Chim Cher-ee

from MARY POPPINS

Words and Music by Richard M. Sherman
and Robert B. Sherman

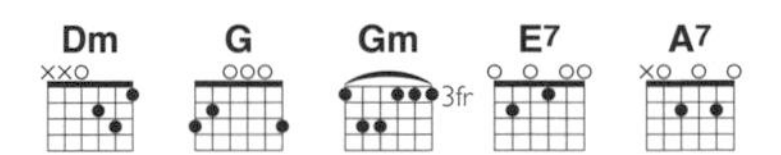

To match original recording, tune guitar down one tone

Chorus 1

```
Dm                                         G
Chim chiminey, chim chiminey, chim chim cher-ee!
 Gm          Dm       E7         A7
A sweep is as lucky as lucky can be.
Dm                                         G
Chim chiminey, chim chiminey, chim chim cher-oo!
     Gm             Dm          A7             Dm
Good luck will rub off when I shakes 'ands with you.
  Gm         Dm       A7         Dm
Or blow me a kiss and that's lucky too.
```

Verse 1

```
Dm                              G
Now, as the ladder of life 'as been strung,
    Gm           Dm           E7           A7
You may think a sweep's on the bottom-most rung.
```

Verse 2

```
         Dm                            G
Though I spend me time in the ashes and smoke,
 Gm          Dm             A7    Dm
In this 'ole wide world there's no 'appier bloke.
```

Chorus 2 *As Chorus 1*

Circle of Life

from THE LION KING

Music by Elton John
Lyrics by Tim Rice

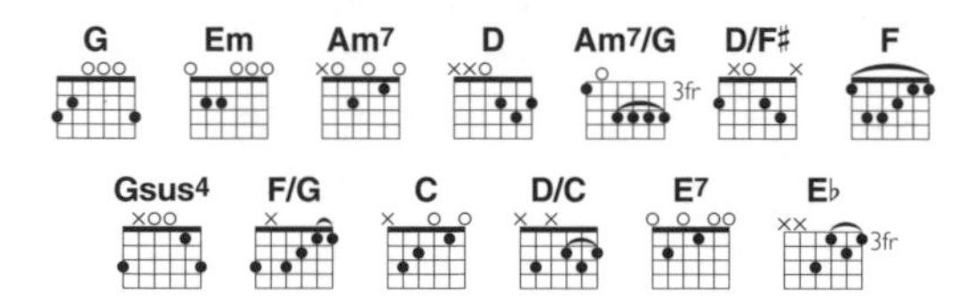

To match original recording, place capo on 3rd fret

Intro ‖: G | Em | Am7 | D :‖

Verse 1

```
               G                          Am7/G
From the day we arrive on the planet
          D/F♯                       G
And blinking, step into the sun,
             Em                          Am7
There's more to see than can ever be seen;
              F                          D
More to do  than can ever be done.

              G                    Am7/G
There's far too much to take in here;
              D/F♯                      G       G/F♯
More to find than can ever be found.
             Em                                 Am7
But the sun rolling high through the sapphire sky
                    F                               D
Keeps great and small on the endless round.
```

```
                                G  Gsus4  G                  F/G
Chorus 1      It's the circle of life,          and it moves us all
                                    C                          D
              Through despair and hope, through faith and love.
                                G       E7                   Am7       E♭
              Till we find our place        on the path un-wind-ing
                        G       D                    C     G
              In the circle,       the circle of life.


Interlude     ‖: G          | Am7         | D          | G          |

              | Em          | Am7         | F          | D          :‖


                                G  Gsus4  G                  F/G
Chorus 2      It's the circle of life,          and it moves us all
                                    C                          D
              Through despair and hope, through faith and love.
                                G       E7                   Am7       E♭
              Till we find our place        on the path un-wind-ing
                        G       D                    C   E♭  G
              In the circle,       the circle of life.
```

The Climb

from HANNAH MONTANA: THE MOVIE

Words and Music by Jessi Alexander and Jon Mabe

E5 Asus2 F♯m7add4 C♯m G♯m B5 B F♯m A

Intro | N.C. | |

```
                E5
*Verse 1*          I can almost see it,

                   That dream I'm dreamin'; but
                Asus2
                   There's a voice inside my head saying
                F♯m7add4
                   "You'll never reach it."
                E5
                   Ev'ry step I'm taking,

                   Ev'ry move I make feels
                Asus2
                Lost with no direction;
                F♯m7add4
                   My faith is shaken.
                   C♯m             G♯m
                But I, I gotta keep try'n;
                      Asus2                    F♯m7add4
                Gotta keep my head held high.
```

Chorus 1

E5
There's always gonna be another mountain;

I'm always gonna wanna make it move.

Asus2
Always gonna be an uphill battle

F♯m7add4 B5
Sometimes, I'm gonna have to lose.

E5
Ain't about how fast I get there;

C♯m B Asus2
Ain't about what's waiting on the side;

E5
It's the climb.

Verse 2

E5
The struggles I'm facing,

The chances I'm taking

Asus2
Sometimes might knock me down, but

F♯m7add4
No, I'm not breaking.

E5
I may not know it, but

These are the moments that

Asus2
I'm gonna remember most, yeah.

F♯m7add4
Just gotta keep going.

C♯m
And I,

G♯m
I gotta be strong,

Asus2 F♯m7add4
Just keep pushing on.

```
              E5
*Chorus 2*    'Cause there's always gonna be another mountain;

                  I'm always gonna wanna make it move.
              Asus2
                  Always gonna be an uphill battle
              F♯m7add4                             B5
                  Sometimes, I'm gonna have to lose.
              E5
                  Ain't about how fast I get there;
                                                   C♯m  B  Asus2
                  Ain't about what's waiting on the side;
                         E5
                  It's the climb.

              E5
*Chorus 3*        There's always gonna be another mountain;

                  I'm always gonna wanna make it move.
              Asus2
                  Always gonna be an uphill battle;
              E          F♯m   G♯m        A   B   C♯m
                  Some-body's gonna have  to lose.

                  Ain't about how fast I get there;
                                                         C♯m  B  Asus2
                  Ain't about what's waiting on the other side;
                         E5          Asus2
                  It's the climb,         yeah.
                        E5                                      Asus2
              Keep on mov-ing, keep climbing; keep the faith, baby.
                                              E5
              It's all about, it's all about the climb.
                                              Asus2   E5
              Keep the faith, keep your faith.
```

Colors of the Wind

from POCAHONTAS

Music by Alan Menken
Lyrics by Stephen Schwartz

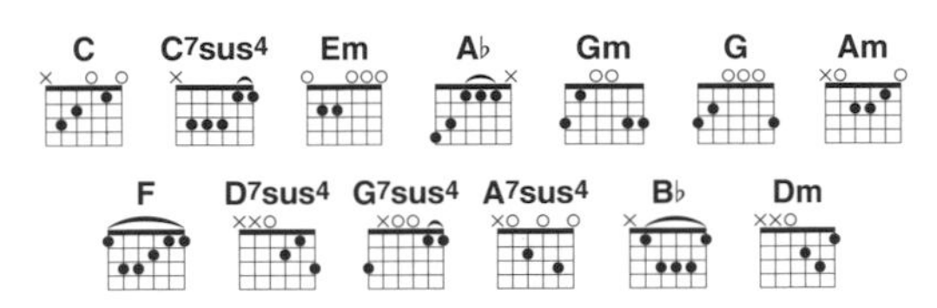

To match original recording, place capo on 1st fret

Intro

        C   C7sus4
You think I'm an ignorant savage,
                    Em
And you've been so many places,
C7sus4
I guess it must be so.
       A♭   Gm   A♭   Gm
But still I cannot see, if the savage one is me,
         C   A♭   G
How can there be so much that you don't know?
N.C.   C   Am   C   Am
You don't know…

Verse 1

        C   Am
You think you own whatever land you land on.
        C   Em
The earth is just a dead thing you can claim.
     Am   F
But I know ev'ry rock and tree and creature
        D7sus4   G7sus4   Am
Has a life, has a spirit, has a name.

Verse 2

```
    C                                      Am
You think the only people who are people
          C                                   Em
Are the people who look and think like you,
   Am                                    F
But if you walk in the footsteps of a stranger
               D7sus4           G7sus4           C
You'll learn things you never knew you never knew.
```

Chorus 1

```
              Am                                 Em       F
Have you ever heard the wolf cry to the blue corn moon,
   Am                                      Em
Or asked the grinning bobcat why he grinned?
           F                 G              C           Am
Can you sing with all the voices of the mountain?
           F                                A7sus4
Can you paint with all the colors of the wind?
         D7sus4          G7sus4        C      Am   C   Am
Can you paint with all the colors of the wind?
```

Verse 3

```
      C                                    Am
Come run the hidden pine trails of the forest,
      C                                      Em
Come taste the sun-sweet berries of the earth.
      Am                           F
Come roll in all the riches all a - round you,
         D7sus4       G7sus4                 Am
And for once never wonder what they're worth.
```

Verse 4

```
    C                                  Am
The rainstorm and the river are my brothers.
    C                             Em
The heron and the otter are my friends.
    Am                              F
And we are all connected to each other
   D7sus4     G7sus4          C
In a circle, in a hoop that never ends.
```

Bridge

```
Em  F              C           Am
How high does the sycamore grow?
        Bb                       F     G
If you cut it down, then you'll never know.
```

Chorus 2

```
              Am                              Em        G
And you'll never hear the wolf cry to the blue corn moon,
    Am                                Em
For whether we are white or copper-skinned,
              F                G              C          Am
We need to sing with all the voices of the mountain,
          F                              A7sus4
Need to paint with all the colors of the wind.
          Dm                 G              Em
You can own the earth and still all you'll own is earth
    F             Am                 F       G      C
Un - til you can paint with all the colors of the wind.
```

Cruella De Vil

from 101 DALMATIANS

Words and Music by Mel Leven

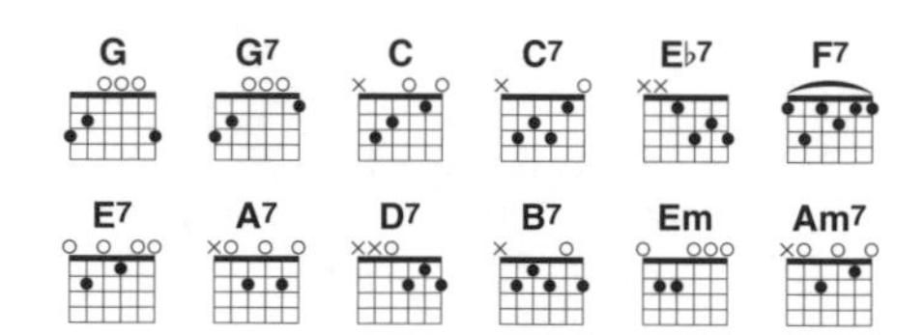

To match original recording, place capo on 1st fret

Verse 1

```
      G          G7            C         C7
Cru-ella De Vil,     Cru-ella De Vil;
  G                G7               C                C7
If she doesn't scare you, no evil thing will.
    G               E♭7                 F7        E7
To see her is to take a sudden     chill.
     A7          D7       G
Cru-ella, Cru-ella De Vil.
```

Verse 2

```
      G              G7        C                 C7
The curl of her lips, the ice in her stare;
    G              G7                C               C7
All innocent children had better beware.
       G                E♭7                  F7      E7
She's like a spider waiting for the    kill.
     A7                  D7       G
Look out for the Cru-ella De Vil.
```

Verse 3

B7 Em
At first, you think Cruella is the devil,
B7 Em
But after time has worn away the shock,
A7
You come to realize you've seen her kind of eyes
E♭7 Am7 D7
Watching you from underneath a rock.

Verse 4

G G7 C C7
This vampire bat, this inhuman beast;
G G7 C C7
She ought to be locked up and never re-leased.
G E♭7 F7 E7
The world was such a wholesome place un-til
A7 D7 G
Cru-ella, Cru-ella De Vil.

Do You Want to Build a Snowman?

from FROZEN

Music and Lyrics by Kristen Anderson-Lopez and Robert Lopez

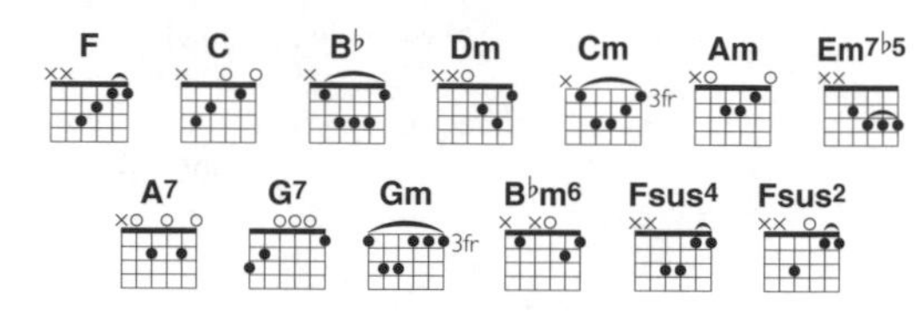

To match original recording, tune guitar down one tone

Verse 1

```
                        F
Do you want to build a snowman?
                        C
Come on, let's go and play!
                B♭
I never see you anymore.
              Dm
Come out the door!
                       Cm
It's like you've gone a-way.
F                      B♭
   We used to be best buddies,
     Am         F
And now we're not.
 Em7♭5           A7      Dm
I wish you would tell me why.
G7   N.C.                    Gm
     Do you want to build a snowman?
                        B♭m6
It doesn't have to be a snowman.

Go away, Anna.
       F    Fsus4   Fsus2
Okay, bye.

| F Fsus4   Fsus2 | F Fsus4   Fsus2 |
```

Go away, Anna.

Verse 2

C N.C. F
Do you want to build a snowman?
C
Or ride our bike around the halls?
B♭
I think some company is overdue;
Dm Cm
I've started talking to the pictures on the walls.
N.C.
Hang in there, Joan!
B♭
It gets a little lonely,
F
All these empty rooms,
A7 Dm
Just watching the hours tick by.

Verse 3

N.C. F
Elsa? Please, I know you're in there.
C
People are asking where you've been.
B♭
They say, 'Have courage,' and I'm trying to;
Dm Am
I'm right out here for you, just let me in.
B♭
We only have each other;
C F
It's just you and me.
Em7♭5 Dm G7
What are we gonna do?
N.C. F
Do you want to build a snowman?

Down to Earth

from WALL-E

Music by Thomas Newman and Peter Gabriel
Words by Peter Gabriel

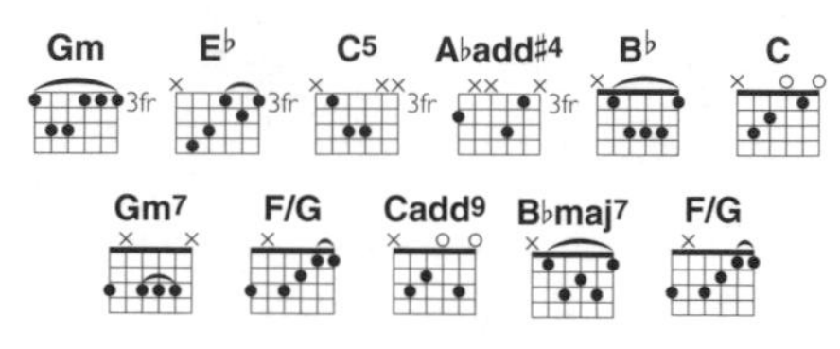

To match original recording, place capo on 1st fret

Intro
| Gm | E♭ | C5 | A♭add♯4 |

||: B♭ | C | B♭ | C :||

Verse 1

B♭ C B♭
Did you think that your feet had been bound
C B♭ C B♭
By what gravity brings to the ground?
C Gm7 E♭
Did you feel you were tricked
Gm7 E♭
By the future you picked?
B♭ C B♭
Well, come on down.
C Gm7 E♭
All those rules don't ap-ply
Gm7 E♭
When you're high in the sky,
B♭
So come on down,
C
Come on down.

```
                          F/G           C
Chorus 1     We're comin' down to the ground;
                      F/G               C
             There's no better place to go.
                     F/G                C
             We've got snow up on the mountains;
                     F/G                C
             We've got rivers down be-low.
                         F/G           C
             We're comin' down to the ground.
                          F/G                 C
             We'll hear the birds sing in the trees,
                   F/G                       C
             And the land will be looked after.
                          F/G                 C
             We'll send the seeds out in the breeze.

             | B♭     | C      | B♭     | C      |

                      B♭               C                 B♭     C
Verse 2      Did you think you'd es-caped from rou-tine
                  B♭            C              B♭       C
             By changing the script and the scene?
                 Gm7          E♭
             Des-pite all you made of it,
                       Gm7              E♭
             You were always afraid
                 B♭      C      B♭      C
             Of a change.
                        Gm7          E♭
             You've got a lot on your chest;
                          Gm7          E♭
             Well, you can come as my guest,
                         B♭      C
             So come on down
                       B♭
             Come on down
```

Chorus 2 *As Chorus 1*

Bridge

```
Cadd9                       B♭
    Like the fish in the ocean,
Bbmaj7                         C
    We felt at home in the sea.
Cadd9                                  B♭
    We learned to live off the good land;
Bbmaj7                              C
    We learned to climb up a tree.
Cadd9                       B♭
    Then we got up on two legs,
Bbmaj7                  C
    But we wanted to fly.
Cadd9                                      B♭
    Oh, when we messed up our homeland,
Bbmaj7                  C
    We set sail for the sky.
```

Chorus 3 *As Chorus 1*

Chorus 4

```
                 F/G
We're comin' down,
C                    F/G
  Comin' down to Earth.
C                 F/G
  Like babies at birth,
C                    F/G
  Comin' down to Earth.
C                 F/G
  Redefine your priorities:
C                   F/G
  These are ex-tra-or-di-nary qualities.

| C              | F/G            |

| C              | F/G            |
```

Chorus 5 *As Chorus 1*

Chorus 6 *As Chorus 4*

A Dream Is a Wish Your Heart Makes

from CINDERELLA

Music by Mack David and Al Hoffman
Lyrics by Jerry Livingston

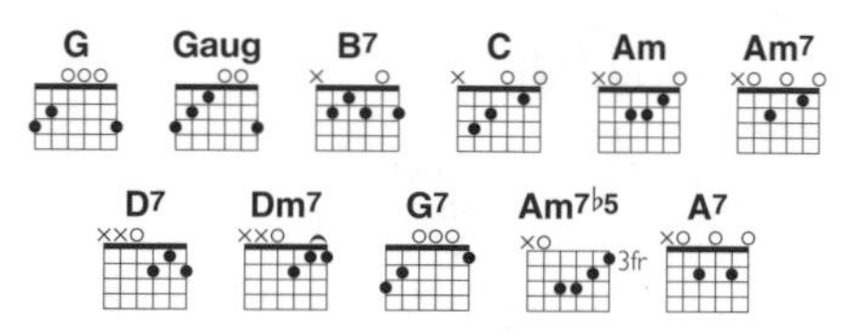

To match original recording, tune guitar down three semitones

Verse

```
  G              Gaug        G                                  B7     C
A dream is a wish your heart makes when you're fast a-sleep.
   Am                              Am7            D7
In dreams you will lose your heartaches,
       Am7                         G
What-ever you wish for, you keep.
                       Gaug          G
Have faith in your dreams and someday
      Dm7            G7                C
Your rainbow will come smiling through.
N.C.        Am                     Am7♭5
No matter how your heart is grieving,
  G                    A7
If you keep on be - lieving,
     Am7              D7               G
The dream that you wish will come true.
```

Evermore

from BEAUTY AND THE BEAST

Music by Alan Menken
Lyrics by Tim Rice

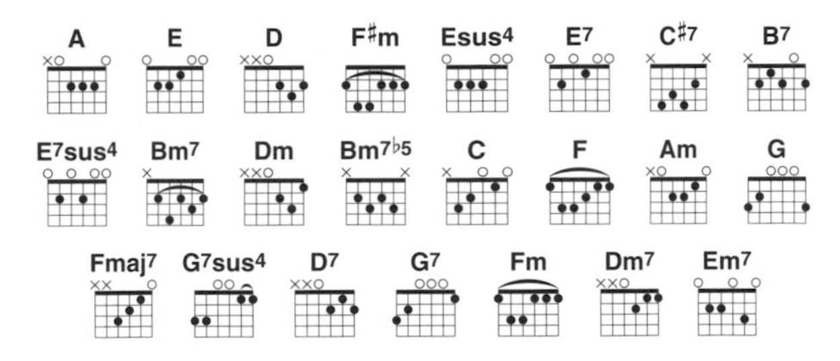

To match original recording, tune guitar down one semitone

Verse 1

```
A                          E     A
   I was the one who had it all;
                                 D
I was the master of my fate.
                  F♯m   E                F♯m
I never needed any - body in my life;
D                  A            Esus4   E
   I learned the truth too late.
A                            E          A
   I'll never shake a-way the pain.
                                          D
I close my eyes, but she's still there.
            F♯m                E              F♯m
I let her steal into my melancholy heart;
D                       A        E        E7
   It's more than I can bear.
```

Chorus 1

D A
Now I know she'll never leave me,
D A
Even as she runs a-way.
D C♯7 F♯m A
She will still tor-ment me, calm me, hurt me,
B7 E7sus4 E
Move me, come what may.
Bm7 A
Wasting in my lonely tower,
D C♯7 F♯m Dm
Waiting by an open door,
A Bm7♭5
I'll fool myself she'll walk right in,
A E7sus4 A
And be with me for ev-er-more.

Verse 2

C G C
I rage against the trials of love.
F
I curse the fading of the light.
Am G Am
Though she's al-ready flown so far beyond my reach,
Fmaj7 C G7sus4
She's never out of sight.

```
                    F                          C
Chorus 2    Now I know she'll never leave me,
            F                              C
            Even as she fades from view.
            F                  E7
            She will still in-spire me,
            Am         C    D7              G7sus4   G7
            Be a part   of ev'rything I do.
            F                           C
            Wasting in my lonely tower,
            F                  E7    Am     Fm      C
            Waiting by an open door,
            Fmaj7                              C
              I'll fool myself she'll walk right in,
            Dm7            Em7                  Am    Em
              And as the long, long nights be-gin,
            Fmaj7           Em7                 Am     D7
              I'll think of all that might have been,
                      C          G7sus4    G     C     Am   F   G7   C
            Waiting here for ev     -      er  -  more.
```

Ev'rybody Wants to Be a Cat

from THE ARISTOCATS

Words by Floyd Huddleston
Music by Al Rinker

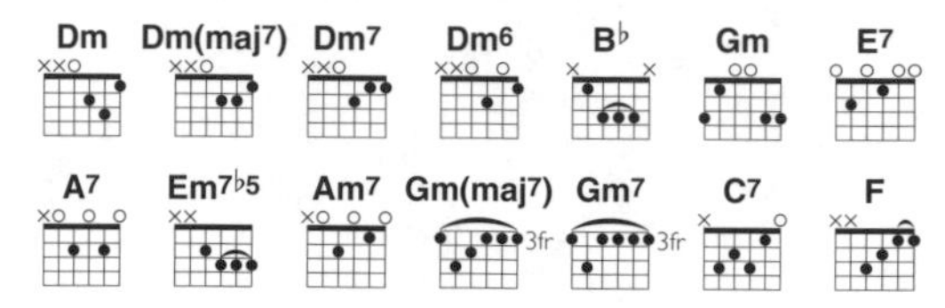

To match original recording, tune guitar down one tone

Verse 1

```
Dm              Dm(maj7)        Dm7       Dm6
Ev'rybody wants to be a cat,
                B♭              Gm
Because a cat's the only cat
      E7                  A7
Who knows where it's at!
Dm              Dm(maj7)
Ev'rybody's pickin' up
          Dm7        Dm6
On that feline beat,
B♭                       Em7♭5       Am7  Dm
  'Cause ev'rything else is ob - so - lete.
```

Bridge 1

```
  Gm                       Gm(maj7)
A square with a horn
               Gm7                       C7
Makes you wish you weren't born
       F
Ev'ry time he plays!
               Em7♭5              A7
But with a square in the act,
           Em7♭5           A7         Dm                Em7♭5  A7
You can set music back   to the caveman days!
```

Verse 2

Dm Dm(maj7) Dm7 Dm6
I've heard some corny birds Who tried to sing,
Bb Gm
But still a cat's the only cat
E7 A7
Who knows how to swing!
Dm Dm(maj7)
Who wants to dig a long-haired gig
Dm7 Dm6
And stuff like that,
Bb Em7b5 Am7 Dm
When ev-'ry-bo-dy wants to be a cat.

Bridge 2 *As Bridge 1*

Verse 3

Dm Dm(maj7) Dm7 Dm6
Ev'rybody wants to be a cat,
Bb Gm
Because a cat's the only cat
E7 A7
Who knows where it's at!
Dm
When playing jazz
Dm(maj7) Dm7 Dm6
You always has a welcome mat,
Bb Em7b5 Am7 Dm
'Cause ev-'ry-bod-y digs a swinging cat!

For the First Time in Forever

from FROZEN

Music and Lyrics by Kristen Anderson-Lopez and Robert Lopez

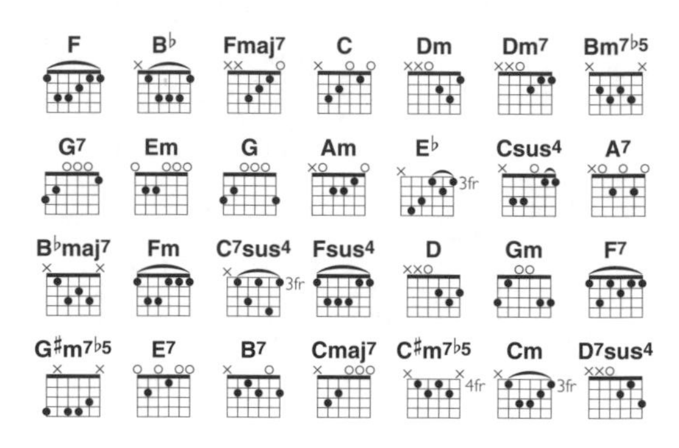

Verse 1

F B♭
Anna: The window is open! So's that door!

Fmaj7 B♭
I didn't know they did that anymore.

F C
Who knew we owned eight thousand salad plates?

F B♭
For years I've roamed these empty halls.

Fmaj7 B♭
Why have a ballroom with no balls?

Dm Dm7 Bm7♭5 G7
Finally, they're op'ning up the gates!

Pre-Chorus 1

Em Fmaj7
There'll be actual real live people;

G Am
It'll be totally strange.

E♭ Csus4 C
But, wow! am I so ready for this change!

Chorus 1

F B♭
'Cause for the first time in for-ev-er,
C F
There'll be music, there'll be light.
Dm Am
For the first time in for-ev-er,
E♭ A7
I'll be dancing through the night.
Dm Dm7
Don't know if I'm elated or gas - sy,
B♭maj7 G7
But I'm somewhere in that zone.
Fm B♭
'Cause for the first time in for-ev-er,
C7sus4 Fsus4
I won't be a-lone.
F Fsus4
I can't wait to meet ev-'ry-one.
F Fsus4 F
What if I meet… …THE one!

Verse 2

B♭
Tonight, imagine me, gown and all,
Fmaj7 B♭
Fetchingly draped a-gainst the wall,
F Csus4 C
The picture of sophisticated grace.
F B♭
I suddenly see him standing there:
Fmaj7 B♭
A beautiful stranger, tall and fair.
Dm Dm7 Bm7♭5 G7
I wanna stuff some choc'late in my face!

Pre-Chorus 2

Em F
But then we laugh and talk all evening,
G Am
Which is totally biz-arre,
E♭ Csus4
Nothing like the life I've led so far.

```
             F                  B♭
Chorus 2     For the first time in for-ev-er,
                 C                          F
             There'll be magic, there'll be fun.
             Dm                 Am
             For the first time in for-ev-er,
                 E♭                      A7
             I could be noticed by someone.
               Dm                 Dm7
             And I know it is totally crazy
                B♭maj7           Bm7♭5
             To dream I'd find ro-mance,
                   Fm                 B♭maj7
             But for the first time in for-ev-er,
             C7sus4                    F
               At least I've got a chance.

             D                              Am
Bridge 1     Elsa:  Don't let them in;  don't let  them see;
             C                                    G     Gm
               Be the good girl you always have to be.
             D          Am         G    C
               Conceal,    don't feel,    put on a show.
                  G                        Gm       D
             Make one wrong move, and ev'ryone will know.

                 C        F                                 F7
Pre-Chorus 3 But it's only for to-day.  Anna: It's only for to-day
                          G                               G7
             Elsa: It's agony to wait!  Anna: It's agony to wait!
                   G♯m7♭5                                E7
             Elsa: Tell the guards to open up  Anna: the gate! The gate!
```

```
                           G                C
Chorus 3    Anna: For the first time in for-ev-er,

            Elsa: Don't let them in; don't let them see.
                              D                     G
            Anna: I'm getting what I'm dreaming of:

            Elsa: Be the good girl you always have to be.
                       Em                  Bm
            Anna: A chance to change my lonely world,

            Elsa: Conceal;
                       F                 B7
            Anna: A chance to find true love.

            Elsa: Conceal, don't feel, don't let them know.
                      Em              Em7         Cmaj7       C#m7b5
            Anna: I know it all ends to-mor-row, so it has to be to-day.
            N.C.              G                Cmaj7
              'Cause for the first time in for-ev-er,
                      G          A7    Cm
            For the first time in for-ev-er,
            D7sus4                      G
              Nothing's in my way!
```

Friend Like Me

from ALADDIN

Music by Alan Menken
Lyrics by Howard Ashman

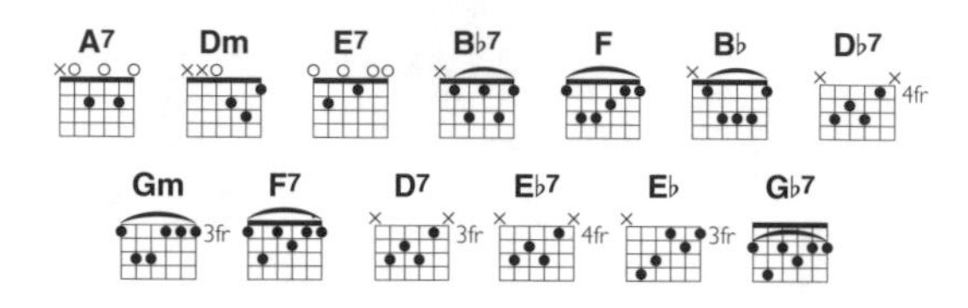

Verse 1

A7 Dm
Well, Ali Baba had them forty thieves.
A7 Dm
Schehera - zade had a thousand tales.
A7 Dm
But, master, you in luck 'cause up your sleeves
E7 A7
You got a brand of magic never fails.
Dm
You got some power in your corner now,
A7 Dm
Some heavy ammunition in your camp.
A7 Dm
You got some punch, pizazz, ya-hoo and how.
E7 A7
See, all you gotta do is rub that lamp.
N.C.
And I'll say…

```
            Dm                Bb7       A7
Chorus 1      Mister A - laddin, sir,
                  Dm            Bb7          A7
            What will your pleasure be?
                      F                          Bb      Db7
              Let me take your order, jot it down.
                      F                               A7  Dm
            You ain't never had a friend like me.
                  Bb7 A7
              No, no, no.
            Dm                  Bb7       A7
              Life is your restau-raunt
                 Dm          Bb7      A7
            And I'm your maître d'.
                    F                        Bb        Db7
            C'mon, whisper what it is you want.
                      F                               A7  Dm
            You ain't never had a friend like me.
                              Bb7
              Yes, sir, we pride ourselves on service.
                            Dm          A7            Dm
            You're the boss, the king, the shah.
               Bb7
            Say what you wish. It's yours!
                                           Gm                      A7
            True dish how 'bout a little more bak-la-va?
            Dm                      Bb7          A7
              Have some of column "A".
               Dm     Bb7          A7
            Try all of column "B".
                   F                     Bb           Db7
              I'm in the mood to help you, dude,
                      F                               A7  Dm
            You ain't never had a friend like me.
```

Interlude

```
Dm         B♭7   A7
Waahah. Oh   my.
Dm         B♭7   A7
Waahah. No,   no.
Dm         B♭7       A7   B♭7  A7
Waahah. Na, na, na.
```

Bridge

```
Dm
  Can your friends do this? Can your friends do that?
                            F7
Can your friends pull this out their little hat?
                            Dm                F
  Can your friends go poof! Well, looky here.
                          A7
Can your friends go abracadabra, let 'er rip
                                          D7
  And then make the sucker dis-ap-pear?
```

Verse 2

```
                D7                     Gm
So don't cha sit there slack-jawed, buggy-eyed.
              D7                        Gm
I'm here to answer all your midday prayers.
              D7             Gm
You got me     bona-fide certified.
            A7                           D7
You got a genie for your chargé d'af-faires.
                             Gm
I got a powerful urge to help you out.
              D7                     Gm
So whatcha wish, I really want to know.
            D7                     Gm
You got a list that's three miles long, no doubt.
                A7                 D7
Well, all you gotta do is rub like so. And oh.
```

```
              Gm           E♭7      D7
*Outro*         Mister A-laddin, sir,
                   Gm                 E♭7      D7
              Have a wish or two or three.
                 B♭                 E♭       G♭7
                I'm on the job, you big na-bob.
                      B♭
                You ain't never had a friend, never had a friend,
                    G♭7
              You ain't never had a friend, never had a friend,
                    E♭7                      D7  Gm    E♭7    D7
              You ain't never had a friend like me.
              Gm        E♭7 D7    Gm         E♭7 D7
              Waahah.             Waahah.
                      E♭7                      D7  Gm
                You ain't never had a friend like me. Ha!
```

Fall on Me

from THE NUTCRACKER AND THE FOUR REALMS

Written by Ian Axel, Chad Vaccarino,
Matteo Bocelli and Fortunato Zampaglione

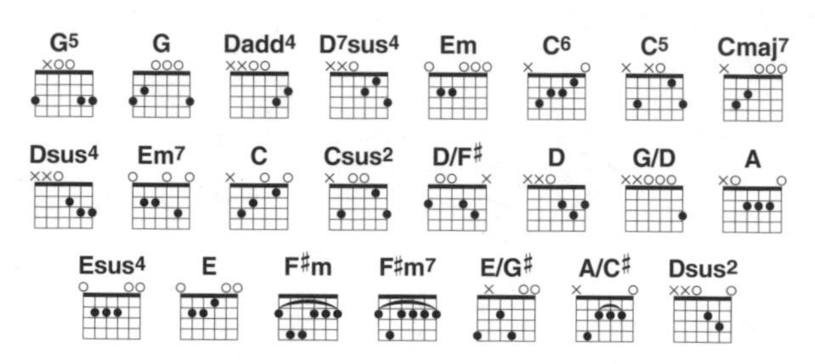

To match original recording, tune guitar down one semitone

Intro | G5 G | Dadd4 | D7sus4 |
| Em | | C6 |

Verse 1

C5 Cmaj7 G5
I thought sooner or later the lights up above
Dsus4
Would come down in circles and guide me to love.
Em7
But I don't know what's right for me.

I cannot see straight.
C
I've been here too long and I don't want to wait for it.
G5
Fly like a cannonball, straight through my soul.
Dsus4
Tear me to pieces and make me feel whole.
Em7
I'm willing to fight for it and carry this weight.
C G5
But with ev'ry step I keep questioning what is true.

Chorus 1

Dadd4 Em7
Fall on me with open arms.
Csus2 G5
Fall on me from where you are.
Csus2 Em7
Fall on me with all your light,
Csus2 G5
With all our light, with all your light.

Verse 2

Presto una luce ti luminerà
Dsus4
Seguila sempre, guidarti saprà.
Em7
Tu non arrenderti, attento a non perderti
Csus2
E il tuo passato avrà senso per te.
G5
Vor-rei che credessi in te stesso, ma sì
Dsus4
In ogni passo che muoverai qui.
Em7 D/F♯ G
E un viaggio infinito sor-ri-de-rò se
Csus2 G5
Nel tempo che fugge mi porti con te.

Chorus 2

Dadd4 Em7
Fall on me ascoltami.
Csus2 G5
Fall on me, abbracciami.
Csus2 Em7
Fall on me, finché vorrai.
Csus2 Em7 D/F♯ G
Finché vorai finché vorrai.
Csus2 Em7 D/F♯ G
Finché vorrai.

```
              D                  G/D        D          C          G
*Bridge*        I close my eyes    and I'm seeing you ev'rywhere.
              D               G/D            D              C          G
                I step outside,    it's like I'm breathing you in the air.
              D  Em7  D/F#                      C       A
                           I can feel you're there.

                           Esus4   E               F#m
*Chorus 3*    Fall on me,              ascoltami.
                           D                 A
              Fall on me,    abbracciami.
                           Esus4                          F#m7
              Fall on me,         with all your light,
                       E/G# A               D            Esus4 A
              With all         your light,  with all               your light.

*Outro*       |          | Esus4  |         | F#m7   |

              | A/C#     | Dsus2  |         | A      |
```

Go the Distance

from HERCULES

Music by Alan Menken
Lyrics by David Zippel

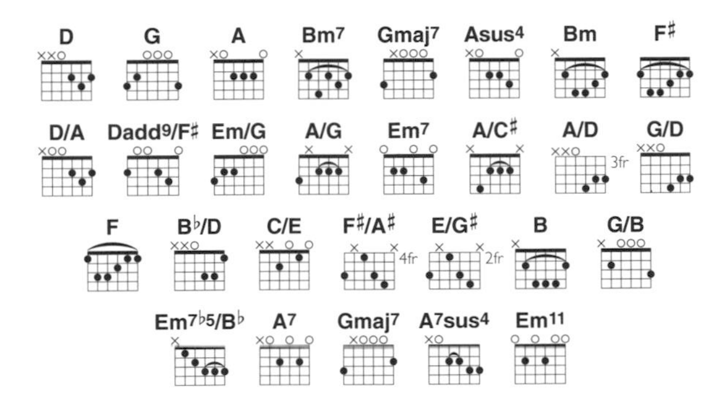

Intro | D | G A D | | G A D | |

Verse 1

G A D G A D
I have of - ten dreamed of a far-off place
G A Bm7 Gmaj7 Asus4 A
Where a he - ro's welcome would be waiting for me,
G A D G A Bm
Where the crowds will cheer when they see my face,
G F♯ Bm D/A G Asus4 A
And a voice keeps saying this is where I'm meant to be.

Chorus 1

Dadd9/F♯ Em/G D/A A A/G
I'll be there someday. I can go the distance.
Dadd9/F♯ Em/G D/A A A/G
I will find my way if I can be strong.
Dadd9/F♯ G Bm7 Em7
I know every mile will be worth my while.
G A D A/C♯ Bm D/A Gmaj7 D A/D G/D
When I go the dis-tance, I'll be right where I be-long.

| D A/D G/D |

Verse 2

G A D G A D
Down an un-known road to em-brace my fate,
G A Bm7 Gmaj7 Asus4 A
Though that road may wander, it will lead me to you.
G A D G A Bm
And a thou-sand years would be worth the wait.
G F♯ Bm D/A G Asus4 A
It might take a lifetime, but some-how I'll see it through.

Chorus 2

Dadd9/F♯ Em/G D/A A A/G
And I won't look back. I can go the distance.
Dadd9/F♯ Em/G D/A A A/G
And I'll stay on track. No, I won't accept de-feat.
Dadd9/F♯ G Bm7 Em7
It's an uphill slope, but I won't lose hope
G A D A/C♯ Bm D/A G Asus4 A D A/D G/D
Till I go the dis-tance and my journey is com-plete.

Bridge

D A/D G/D
Oh, yeah.
F B♭/D C/E A/C♯
But to look beyond the glory is the hardest part,
D G F♯/A♯
For a hero's strength is measured by his heart.

Instru | E/G♯ F♯/A♯ B | E/G♯ F♯/A♯ B | G/B A/C♯ D |

| Bm Em7♭5/B♭ | D/A | G A7 |

Chorus 3

```
         Dadd9/F♯      Em/G D/A            A         G
Like a shooting star,         I will go the distance.
         Dadd9/F♯            Em/G  D/A             A       G
I will search the world.         I will face its harms.
       Dadd9/F♯                  E/G♯  F♯/A♯         Bm
I         don't care how far.           I can go the distance
         G    A   D   A/C♯ Bm  D/A   G         Asus4 A       D
Till I find my he-ro's   wel-come waiting in            your arms.
```

| D Asus4 |

```
         Dadd9/F♯            Gmaj7          Bm7    Em11
I will search the world.           I will face its harms
         G    A   D  A/C♯ Bm  D/A   G         A7sus4        G/B  A/C♯ D
Till I find my he-ro's  wel-come waiting in          your arms.
```

God Help the Outcasts

from THE HUNCHBACK OF NOTRE DAME

Music by Alan Menken
Lyrics by Stephen Schwartz

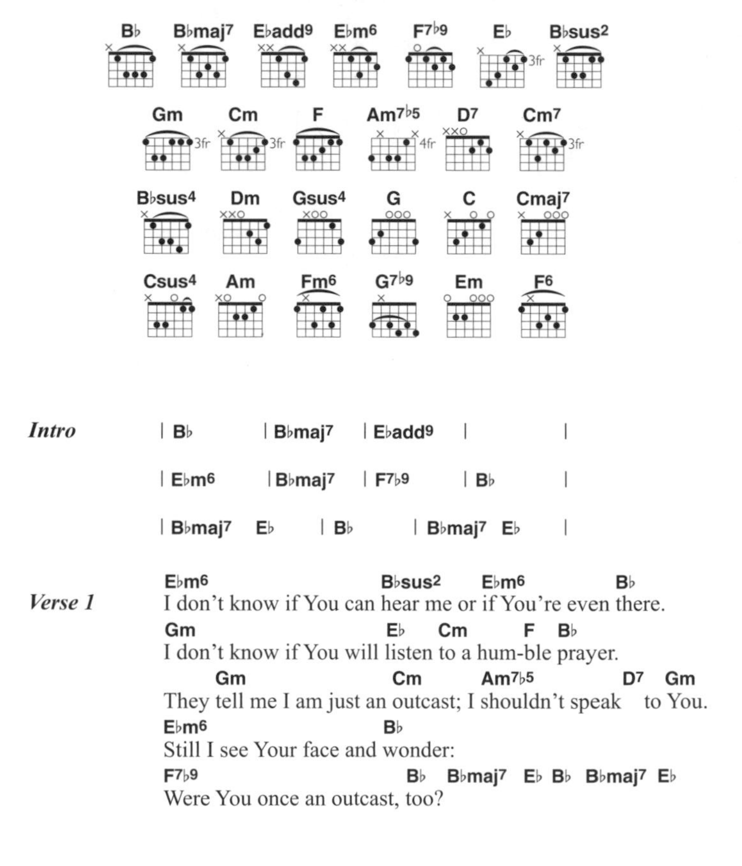

Intro

B♭	B♭maj7	E♭add9	
E♭m6	B♭maj7	F7♭9	B♭
B♭maj7 E♭	B♭	B♭maj7 E♭

Verse 1

```
E♭m6                           B♭sus2      E♭m6            B♭
I don't know if You can hear me or if You're even there.
Gm                              E♭     Cm         F   B♭
I don't know if You will listen to a hum-ble prayer.
        Gm                       Cm          Am7♭5               D7   Gm
They tell me I am just an outcast; I shouldn't speak    to You.
E♭m6                             B♭
Still I see Your face and wonder:
F7♭9                               B♭   B♭maj7  E♭  B♭  B♭maj7  E♭
Were You once an outcast, too?
```

Verse 2

B♭ B♭maj7 E♭add9
God help the outcasts, hungry from birth.
Cm7 F B♭sus4 B♭
Show them the mercy they don't find on Earth.
Gm F Cm7
The lost and forgotten, they look to You still.
E♭m6 B♭ F7♭9 B♭ B♭maj7 E♭ B♭ F E♭
God help the outcasts or nobody will.

Verse 3

B♭ B♭maj7 E♭add9
I ask for nothing, I can get by.
Cm7 F B♭sus4 B♭
But I know so many less lucky than I.
Gm F Cm7
God help the outcasts, the poor and down-trod.
E♭m6 B♭ F7♭9 B♭ F
I thought we all were the children of God.

Bridge

E♭ B♭ Cm
I don't know if there's a reason why some are blessed,
B♭ Dm
some not.
Gm E♭add9
Why the few You seem to favor,
Cm7 B♭ Dm Gsus4 G
They fear us, flee us, try not to see us.

Verse 4

```
C                  Cmaj7         F
God help the outcasts, the tattered, the torn,
Dm          G           Csus4  C          G
Seeking an answer to why       they were born.
Am                              Dm
Winds of misfortune have blown them about.
Fm6              C   Cmaj7  G7♭9           Am   Cmaj7
You made the out-casts;    don't cast them out.
     Fm6          C          Fm6          C
The poor and un-lucky, the weak and the odd;
Fm6  C        Dm   C         G7♭9        C
I    thought we    all were children of God.
```

```
| Cmaj7   F   | C         | Cmaj7   F   | Am        |

| Em          | F6        | G           | C         |
```

Hawaiian Roller Coaster Ride

from LILO & STITCH

Words and Music by Alan Silvestri and Mark Keali'i Ho'omalu

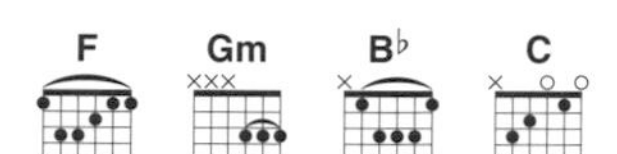

Intro

```
   N.C.
‖: Aloha, e, aloha e, (Aloha e, aloha e.)

   Ano'ai ke aloha e. (Ano'ai ke aloha e.) :‖

‖: F      Gm     | F              :‖
```

Verse 1

```
F                                 Gm
There's no place I'd rather be
F
(Than on my surfboard out at sea.)
                                Gm
Lingering in the ocean blue.
F
(And if I had one wish come true)
    B♭                        F     B♭
I'd surf 'till the sun sets   be-yond the horizon.
F                         Gm
(Awikiwiki, mai lohi-lohi.
F
Lawe mai i ko papa he'e nalu.)
C                            B♭                       F    Gm     F
   Flying by on a Ha - waiian roller coaster ride.
```

```
          F
Chorus    Awikiwiki, mai lohilohi.
          B♭                F
          (Lawe mai i ko papa he'e nalu.)

          Pi'i na lulu la lahalaha.
          B♭                F
          (O   ka moana hanupanupa.)
          C
          Lalala i ka la hanahana.
              B♭
          (Me   ke kai hoene i ka pu'e one.)
          F
          Helehele mai kakou e.
          N.C.
          (Hawaiian roller coaster ride.)

          F                           Gm
Verse 2   There's no place I'd rather be
          F
          (Than on the seashore dry, wet and free.)
                                        Gm
          On golden sand is where I'd lay,
          F
          (And if I only had my way)
             B♭                     F    B♭
          I'd play 'till the sun sets   be-yond the horizon.
          F                   Gm
          (Lalala i ka la hana-hana.)
              F
          Me   ke kai hoene i ka pu'e one.
          C                        B♭                  F     Gm    F
            It's time to try the Ha-waiian roller coaster ride.
```

Bridge

F
Hang loose, hang ten, how's it shake-a-shaka?
B♭   F
No worry, no fear. Ain't no biggie, brahda.

Puttin' in, cuttin' up, cuttin' back, cuttin' out.
B♭   F
Front side, back side, goofy-footed wipeout.
C
Let's go jumpin', surf's up and pumpin'.
B♭
Coastin' with the motion of the ocean.
F
Whirlpools swinging, cascading, swirling.
N.C.
Hawaiian roller coaster ride.

Slide Gtr Solo *As Verse 1 (Instrumental)*

Banjo Solo

F Gm	F	Gm	F
B♭ F	B♭	F Gm	F
C	B♭	F Gm	F
Gm	F

Verse 3 *As Verse 1*

Outro-Chorus *As Chorus*

Hakuna Matata

from THE LION KING

Music by Elton John
Lyrics by Tim Rice

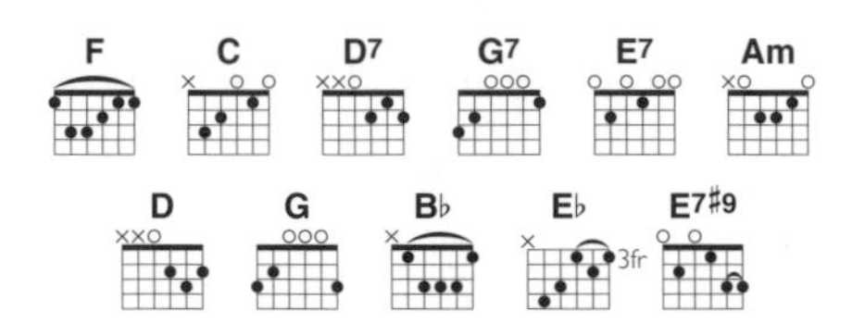

Chorus 1

N.C. F C
Timon: Hakuna ma-tata…what a wonderful phrase!
F D7 G7
Pumbaa: Hakuna ma-tata… ain't no passing craze.
E7 Am C F D
Timon: It means no worries for the rest of your days.
C G
Timon & Pumbaa: It's our problem-free phi-losophy.
N.C. C
Timon: Hakuna ma-tata.

Verse

B♭ F C
Timon: Why, when he was a young wart-hog…
B♭ F C
Pumbaa: When I was a young wart-hog!
N.C.
Timon: Very nice. Pumbaa: Thanks.
E♭ F
Timon: He found his aroma lacked a certain appeal.
C G
He could clear the savannah after ev'ry meal!
B♭ F C
Pumbaa: I'm a sensitive soul, though I seem thick-skinned.
E♭ F G
And it hurt that my friends never stood down wind!

Chorus 2

N.C. F
Timon & Pumbaa: Hakuna ma-tata…

C
what a wonderful phrase!

F D7 G7
Pumbaa: Hakuna ma-tata… ain't no passing craze.

E7♯9 Am C F D
Simba: It means no worries for the rest of your days.

C G
Timon & Simba: It's our problem-free phi-losophy.

N.C. C
Hakuna ma-tata.

F G
All: Hakuna matata. Hakuna matata. Hakuna matata.

E7♯9 Am C F D
Simba: It means no worries for the rest of your days.

C G
Timon & Simba: It's our problem-free phi-losophy.

N.C. C F
Hakuna ma-tata. Hakuna ma-tata.

Outro

G C F
‖: Hakuna ma-tata. Hakuna ma-tata. :‖ *Repeat and fade*

He's a Tramp

from LADY AND THE TRAMP

Words and Music by Peggy Lee and Sonny Burke

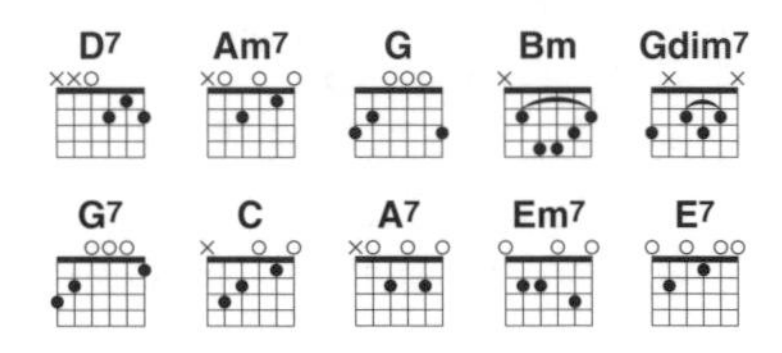

Verse 1

D7 Am7 D7
He's a tramp, but they love him.
Am7 G D7 Am7
Breaks a new heart ev'ry-day.
Bm D7 G
He's a tramp, they a-dore him
Gdim7 D7 G
And I only hope he'll stay that way.

Verse 2

D7 Am7 D7
He's a tramp, he's a scoundrel,
Am7 G D7 Am7
He's a rounder, he's a cad,
Bm D7 G
He's a tramp, but I love him.
Gdim7 D7 G
Yes, even I have got it pretty bad.

```
                   G7
Bridge      You can never tell when he'll show up.
            C
               He gives you plenty of trouble.
            A7                      Em7
               I guess he's just a no 'count pup.
                      E7          Am7      D7
               But I wish that he were double.

                            Am7          D7
Outro       He's a tramp,       he's a rover
            Am7               G           D7          Am7
               And there's nothing more to say.
                      Bm        D7            G
            If he's a tramp,        he's a good one
                    Am7                    D7          G
            And I wish that I could travel his way.
```

How Far I'll Go

from MOANA

Music and Lyrics by Lin-Manuel Miranda

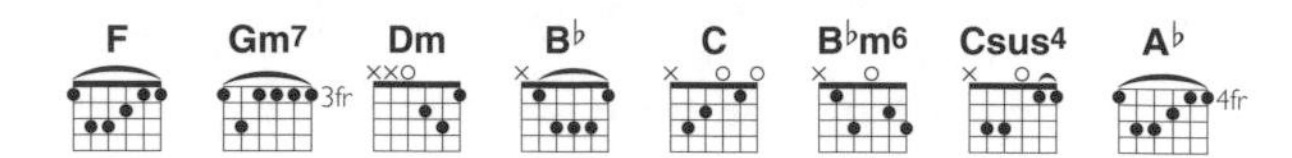

To match original recording, tune guitar down one tone

Verse 1

```
F                                   Gm7
I've been staring at the edge of the water
                 Dm                                 B♭
Long as I can re-mem-ber, never really knowing why.
F                            Gm7
I wish I could be the perfect daughter,
                            Dm                            B♭
But I come back to the water no matter how hard I try.
```

Pre-Chorus 1

```
     Dm
Ev'ry turn I take, ev'ry trail I track,
     C
Ev'ry path I make, Ev'ry road leads back
       F
To the place I know where I cannot go,
         B♭m6
Where I long to be.
```

Chorus 1

```
        F                                         Csus4
See the line where the sky meets the sea, It calls      me,
     C       Dm                B♭
And no one knows how far it goes.
     F                                         Csus4
If the wind in my sail on the sea stays behind      me,
     C       Dm          B♭m6                                     F
One day I'll know. If I go, there's just no telling how far I'll go.
```

Verse 2

Gm7 Dm
I know ev'rybody on this island seems so happy on this island.
B♭
Ev'rything is by de-sign.
F Gm7 Dm
I know ev'rybody on this island has a role on this island,
B♭ F
So maybe I can roll with mine.

Pre-Chorus 2

Dm
I can lead with pride, I can make us strong.
C
I'll be satisfied if I play along,
F
But the voice inside sings a diff'rent song.
B♭m6
What is wrong with me?

Chorus 2

F Csus4
See the light as it shines on the sea: it's blind - ing,
C Dm B♭
But no one knows how deep it goes.
F Csus4
And it seems like it's calling out to me, so come find me
C Dm B♭m6
And let me know. What's be-yond that line? Will I cross that line?

Chorus 3

F Csus4
The line where the sky meets the sea, it calls me,
C Dm B♭
And no one knows how far it goes.
F Csus4
If the wind in my sail on the sea stays behind me,
C Dm F A♭ C
One day I'll know how far I'll go!

I Believe

from A WRINKLE IN TIME

Words and Music by Khaled Khaled, Demi Lovato,
Denisia Andrews and Brittany Coney

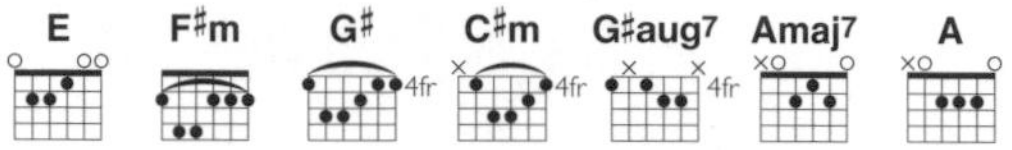

E F♯m G♯ C♯m G♯aug7 Amaj7 A

Intro
E F♯m G♯ C♯m
Ooh, yeah.
E F♯m G♯ C♯m
Ooh.

Verse 1
E F♯m G♯ C♯m
Some people stay and some people move.
E F♯m G♯ C♯m
Tough times don't last, but tough people do.
E F♯m G♯ C♯m
As long as you've got hope, you'll find your way.
E F♯m G♯
There's power in the thoughts that you think,
C♯m
There's power in the words you say.

Pre-Chorus 1
E F♯m G♯ C♯m
Like 'I can, I can, I will, I will.'
E F♯m G♯ C♯m
I am, I am, no fear, no fear.

Chorus 1
E F♯m G♯ C♯m
Today I saw a rainbow in the rain.
E F♯m G♯ C♯m
It told me I can do anything
E F♯m
If I be-lieve, I believe, I be-lieve in me.
G♯ C♯m
I be-lieve, I believe, I be-lieve in me.
E F♯m G♯ C♯m
Ooh, yeah.
E F♯m G♯ C♯m N.C.
Ooh.

```
              E             F♯m  G♯            C♯m
Verse 2         I got the light    inside of me,
              E                     F♯m    G♯                C♯m
                And I've got no choice     but to let it breathe.
              E          F♯m
              As long as    there is love,
              G♯                     C♯m
                I can make it any-where I go.
              E       F♯m
                      If I follow my dreams,
              G♯                       C♯m
              I'll end up building a yellow brick road.

              E                 F♯m           G♯          C♯m
Pre-Chorus 2    Like I can, I can, I will, I will.
              E            F♯m              G♯      C♯m
                I am, I am, no fear, no fear.
```

Chorus 2 *As Chorus 1*

```
              C♯m                G♯aug7
Bridge          I'm living my best life,
              Amaj7                                       C♯m
              I am a flower that's blooming like roses in spring.
                         G♯aug7
              Living my best life,
              Amaj7                                     C♯m
              I am wearing a crown that's only fit for a queen.
                  G♯aug7   A           C♯m
              I'm glorious,     vic-tor-ious,
                 G♯aug7    A
              A warrior.
```

Chorus 3

```
E    F♯m  G♯     C♯m  E              F♯m               G♯    C♯m
   To   -   day                I saw a rainbow in the rain.
E               F♯m      G♯        C♯m
   It told me I can do anything
         E                       F♯m
If I be-lieve, I believe, I be-lieve in me.
      G♯                     C♯m
I be-lieve, I believe, I be-lieve in me.
```

Interlude

```
E                    F♯m           G♯      C♯m
   When times got hard, I went harder.
               E                      F♯m       G♯
Best thing I ever did was believe     in me.
      C♯m
I be-lieve.
```

Chorus 4

```
E    F♯m  G♯     C♯m  E              F♯m               G♯    C♯m
   To   -   day                I saw a rainbow in the rain.
E               F♯m      G♯        C♯m
   It told me I can do anything
         E                       F♯m
If I be-lieve, I believe, I be-lieve in me.
      G♯                     C♯m
I be-lieve, I believe, I be-lieve in me.
```

Outro

```
E               F♯m     G♯                  C♯m
        To suc-ceed,          you must be-lieve
               E
(We the best music.)
      F♯m
I be-lieve.
          G♯
(Another one.)
               C♯m
A wrinkle in time.
```

I Just Can't Wait to Be King

from THE LION KING

Music by Elton John
Lyrics by Tim Rice

To match original recording, tune guitar down one tone

```
Intro      ‖: G       | C    G  |         | D        :‖

                           G
Verse 1    Simba: I'm gonna be a mighty king, so enemies beware!
                            C
           Zazu: Well, I've never seen a king of beasts with
                                   G
                quite so little hair.

           Simba: I'm gonna be the mane event, like no king was before.
              C                                            G
           I'm brushing up on looking down. I'm working on my roar!

                 Am                            G      D     N.C.
Chorus 1   Zazu: Thus far, a rather uninspiring thing.
                        C7       D        G
           Simba: Oh, I just can't wait to be king!
                   C                      G
           Zazu:  You've rather a long way to go, young Master!
                 N.C.
                 If you think...
```

Bridge 1

C
Simba: No one saying "do this,"

Zazu: Now when I said that I...

Am
Simba: No one saying "be there,"

Zazu: What I meant was that the...

D
Simba: No one's saying "stop that,"

Zazu: But what you don't realize...

G
Simba: No one saying "see here."

Zazu: Now see here!

C G Am Cmaj7 D
Simba: Free to run a-round all day,

Zazu: Well, that's definitely out.

C7 D G
Simba: Free to do it all my way!

Verse 2

G
Zazu: I think it's time that you and I arranged a heart to heart.
C G
Simba: Kings don't need advice from little hornbills, for a start.

Zazu: If this is where the monarchy is headed, count me out!
C G
Out of service, out of Africa. I wouldn't hang about.

Chorus 2

Am G D N.C.
Zazu: This child is getting wildly out of wing.
C7 D G
Simba: Oh, I just can't wait to be king!

Bridge 2

C Am
Simba: Ev'rybody look left. *Nala:* Ev'rybody look right.
D
Simba: Ev'rywhere you look I'm
G
Simba & Nala: Standing in the spotlight.

Zazu: Not yet.

C G Am Cmaj7 D
Simba & Nala: Let ev'ry creature go for broke and sing.
C G Am Cmaj7 D
Let's hear it in the herd and on the wing.
C G Am Cmaj7 D
It's gonna be King Simba's finest fling.

Outro-Chorus

C7 D G
Simba: Oh, I just can't wait to be king.
C7 D G
Oh, I just can't wait to be king.
C7 D N.C. G
Oh, I just can't wait to be king!

I See the Light

from TANGLED

Music by Alan Menken
Lyrics by Glenn Slater

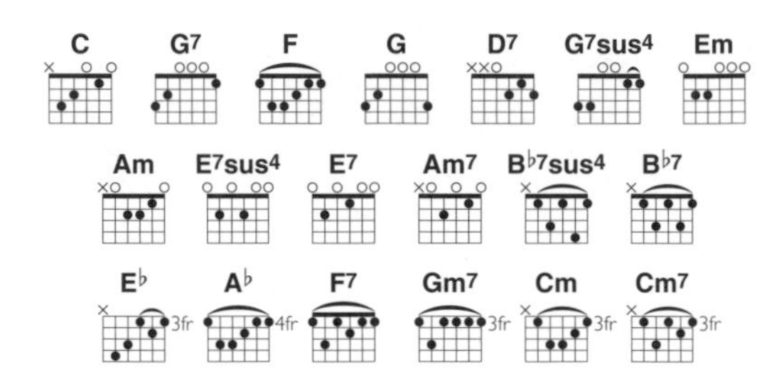

Verse 1

```
C
All those days,
G7                    C
Watching from the windows.

All those years
G7               C
Outside, looking in.
F
All that time,
C            F     G
Never even know-ing
C         D7          G7sus4  G7
Just how blind I've been.
```

Verse 2

```
C
Now I'm here,
G7               C
Blinking in the starlight.

Now I'm here;
G7          C
Suddenly I see.
F
Standing here,
    Em
It's oh, so clear
     Am          D7        G7sus4 G
I'm where I'm meant to be.
```

Chorus 1

```
         F              C
And at last I see the light,
          G7                 C
And it's like the fog has lifted.
         F              C
And at last I see the light,
          E7sus4 E7     Am7
And it's like the sky is new.
          F                      C
And it's warm and real and bright,
          Em                      F
And the world has somehow shifted
C
All at once,
G7                 C
Ev'rything looks diff'rent,
F         G7    C     B♭7sus4     B♭7
Now that I see you.
```

Verse 3

```
E♭
All those days,
B♭7                 E♭
Chasing down a daydream

All those years,
B♭7          E♭
Living in a blur.
A♭
All that ime,
E♭             A♭  B♭7
Never truly see-ing
E♭       F7                  B♭7sus4  B♭7
Things     the way they were.
```

Verse 4

E♭
Now she's here,
B♭7 E♭
Shining in the starlight.

Now she's here;
B♭7 E♭
Suddenly I know:
A♭
If she's here,
Gm7
It's crystal clear
Cm F7 B♭7sus4 B♭
I'm where I'm meant to go.

Chorus 2

A♭ E♭
And at last I see the light,
B♭7sus4 B♭ E♭
And it's like the fog has lifted.
A♭ E♭
And at last I see the light,
G7sus4 G Cm
And it's like the sky is new.
A♭ E♭
And it's warm and real and bright,
Gm7 A♭
And the world has somehow shifted.

Outro

E♭
All at once,
B♭7 E♭
Ev'rything is diff'rent,
A♭ B♭7 E♭ Cm7 F7
Now that I see you.
B♭7sus4 B♭7 E♭
Now that I see you.

I Won't Say (I'm in Love)

from HERCULES

Music by Alan Menken
Lyrics by David Zippel

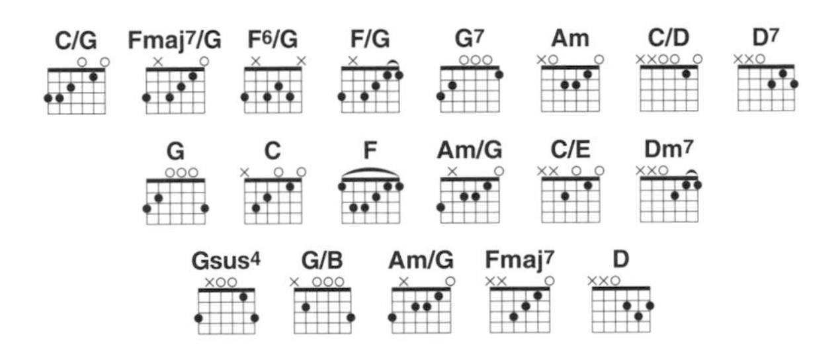

Verse 1

C/G   Fmaj7/G F6/G
If there's a prize for rotten judge - ment,
C/G   F/G G7
I guess I've already won that.
Am   C/D D7
No man is worth the ag-gra-va - tion.
N.C.   F/G G7   F/G G
That's ancient history, been there, done that.

Bridge 1

C
Who d'ya think you're kiddin',
        F   G
He's the Earth and heaven to you.
C
Try to keep it hidden,
      Am   Am/G
Hon-ey, we can see right through you.
F
Girl, ya can't conceal it,
  C/E
We know how ya feel and
               Dm7   Gsus4 G   C
Who you're thinking of.

Chorus 1

```
C
No chance, no way,
              G/B   Am
I won't say it, no,   no.

You swoon,    you sigh.
              Am/G  Fmaj7
Why deny it? Uh      oh.

It's too cliché,
          G           C    C/G   G7
I won't say I'm in love.
```

Verse 2

```
C                                   Fmaj7
  I thought my heart had learned its lesson.
C/E                                G7
  It feels so good when you start    out.
Am                               C/D   D
  My head is screaming, get a grip, girl,
G                            F/G G7   F/G  G
  Unless you're dying to cry  your heart out.
```

Bridge 2

```
C
You keep on denying
      F             G
Who    you are and how you're feeling.
C
Baby, we're not buying.
     Am
Hon,    we saw you hit the ceiling.
F
Face it like a grown-up,
      C/E
When     ya gonna own up
         Dm7                    G7
That ya got, got it, got it bad?
```

```
                C
Chorus 2        No chance, no way,
                             G/B  Am
                I won't say it, no,   no.

                Give up, give in.
                                          Am/G  Fmaj7
                Check the grin, you're in        love.

                This scene won't play,
                                G7
                I won't say I'm in love.
                                                           C
                You're doin' flips, read our lips: you're in love.

                C
Chorus 3        You're way off base,
                             G/B   Am
                I won't say it.

                Get off my case,
                             Am/G  Fmaj7
                I won't say it.

                Girl, don't be proud,
                                C        Am      Fmaj7
                It's O.K. you're in love.
                G7
                Oh, at least out loud,
                                C
                I won't say I'm in love.
```

I Wan'na Be Like You
(The Monkey Song)
from THE JUNGLE BOOK

Words and Music by Richard M. Sherman and Robert B. Sherman

Cm G7 C7 E♭ F7 B♭7 C D D♭

Verse 1

```
 Cm                                      G7
Now I'm the king of the swingers, oh, the jungle V.I.P.
I reached the top and had to stop,
                              Cm
    and that's what's bothering me.
                                                G7
I wanna be a man, mancub, and stroll right into town
And be just like the other men;
                              Cm
    I'm tired of monkeyin' around.
```

Chorus 1

```
B♭7 E♭
Oh, oobee doo,
               C7
I wanna be like you-ou-ou.
          F7            B♭7          E♭
I wanna walk like you, talk like you too.
B♭7              E♭                      C7
   You'll see it's true-ue-ue: an ape like me-ee-ee
     F7           B♭7          E♭    B♭7
Can learn to be human too
```

```
              Cm
Verse 2       Now don't try to kid me, mancub;
                                  G7
              I made a deal with you.

              What I desire is man's red fire
                                         Cm
              To make my dream come true.

              Now give me the secret, mancub;
                                            G7
              Come on, clue me what to do.

              Give me the power of man's red flower
                                    Cm
              So I can be like you.

              B♭7   E♭
Chorus 2      Yeah, oo-bee doo,
                                 C7
              I wanna be like you-ou-ou.
                     F7            B♭7          E♭
              I wana walk like you, talk like you too.
              B♭7          E♭
              You'll see it's true-ue-ue:
                               C7
              Someone like me-ee-ee
                    F7        B♭7          E♭    D    D♭    C
              Can learn to be someone like me.

                     F7        B♭7              E♭    D    D♭    C
Outro         I can learn to be like someone like you.
                     F7        B♭7              E♭
              I can learn to be like someone like me.
```

If I Didn't Have You

from MONSTERS, INC.

Music and Lyrics by Randy Newman

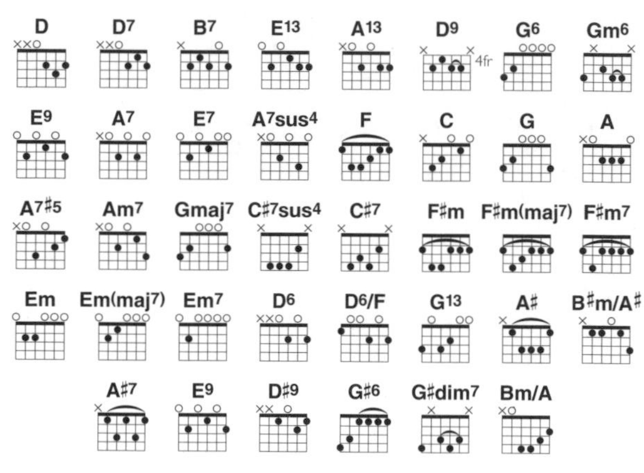

Capo on fret 1

Intro | D D7 B7 | E13 A13 |

Verse 1

D D9
If I were a rich man
G6 Gm6
With a million or two,
D B7
I'd live in a pent - house
E9 A7
In a room with a view.
D D9
And if I were hand - some, *No way!* (*It could happen,*)
G6 Gm6
'Cause dreams do come true,
D B7 E7
I wouldn't have nothin'
A7sus4 D
If I didn't have you.

F C
Wouldn't have nothin'

G
If I didn't have,

F C G
Wouldn't have nothin'

If I didn't have,

F C A A7♯5
Wouldn't have nothin'.

Verse 2

D D9
For years I have en-vied *You green with it*

G6 Gm6
Your grace and your charm.

D B7 E7
Ev'ryone loves you, you know.

A7
Yes, I know, I know, I know.

D D9
But I must ad-mit it,

G6 Gm6
Big guy, you always come through.

D B7 E9
I wouldn't have nothing

A7sus4 D Am7 D7
If I didn't have you.

Bridge 1

G Gmaj7 C♯7sus4 C♯7
You and me to - gether,

F♯m
That's how it

F♯m(maj7) F♯m7 B7
Always should be.

Em Em(maj7) Em7
One with-out the other

A D6
Don't mean nothing to me,

A7♯5
Nothing to me.

Verse 3

D D9
Yeah, I wouldn't be nothin'

Aw, man.

G6 Gm6
If I didn't have you to serve.

D B7
I'm just a punky little eyeball

E7 A7
And a funky optic nerve.

D D9
Hey, I never told you this.

G6 Gm6
Sometimes I get a little blue *(looks good on you)*

D B7 E9
But I wouldn't have nothing

A7sus4 D
If I didn't have you.

Am7 D9
Let's dance!

Bridge 2

Gmaj7 C♯7sus4 C♯7 F♯m F♯m(maj7)
Look, Ma, I'm dan-cing!

F♯m7 B7
Would you let me lead?

Em Em(maj7) Em7
Look at that. It's true!

A7 D
Big guys are light on their feet.

A
Don't you dare dip me.

Don't you dare dip me.

Don't you dare dip me.

Ow! I should've stretched.

D6 D9
Yes, I wouldn't be nothin'

G6 Gm6
If I didn't have you.

I know what you mean Sulley, because...

Verse 4

D B7
I wouldn't know where to go,

Me too, because I

E9 A7sus4
Wouldn't know what to do.

Why do you keep singing my part?

D6 D9
I don't have to say it.

I'll say it anyway 'cause we

G6 Gm6
Both know it's true.

D B7 E9
I wouldn't have nothin'

A7sus4
If I didn't have,

D B7 E9
I wouldn't have nothin'

A7sus4
If I didn't have,

D B7 E9
I wouldn't have nothin'

A7sus4 D6
If I didn't have you.

F C
Wouldn't have nothin'

G D
If I didn't have you.

A7 Bm/A A7
One more time. It worked!

D6 D9
Don't have to say it

Where'd everybody come from?

G6 Gm6
'Cause we both know it's true.

Let's take it home big guy!

```
D       B7                     E7
        I wouldn't have nothing
        A7sus4
If I didn't have,
D       B7                     E7
        I wouldn't have nothing
        A7sus4
If I didn't have,
D       B7                     E7
        I wouldn't have nothing
        A7sus4       D6     D6/F♯
If I didn't have            you.
G13     G♯dim7 Bm/A         E7    A7sus4 D
You.    You.   A, E, I, O that means  you, yeah.
```

I'll Make a Man Out of You

from MULAN

Music by Matthew Wilder
Lyrics by David Zippel

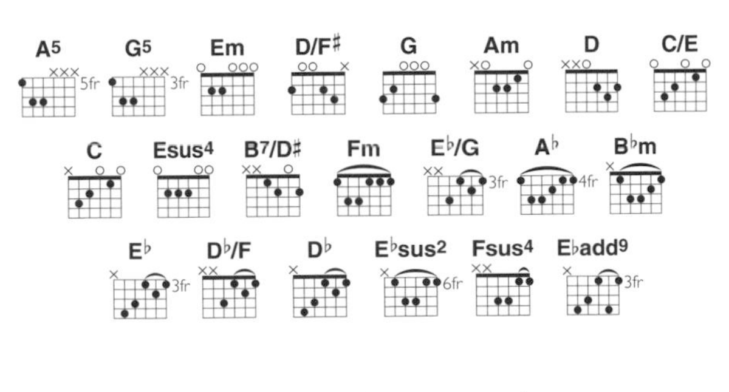

Intro | A5 | G5 |

Verse 1

Em D/F♯ G
Let's get down to bus'ness
Am D
To de-feat the Huns.
Em D/F♯ G
Did they send me daughters
Am D/F♯
When I asked for sons?

Chorus 1

C/E D/F♯
You're the saddest bunch I ever met.
G C
But you can bet before we're through,
D Em D
Mister, I'll make a man of you.

Verse 2

Em D/F♯ G
Tranquil as a forest,
Am D
But on fire with-in.
Em D/F♯ G
Once you find your center
Am D/F♯
You are sure to win.

Chorus 2

```
              C/E                D/F♯
You're a spineless, pale, pa-thetic lot
              G           C
And you haven't got a clue.
                           D            Em       Esus4
Somehow I'll make a man out of you.
```

Bridge

```
C                        D
   I'm never gonna catch my breath.
B7/D♯                          Em
Say goodbye to those who knew me.
D/F♯                  G                    C
Boy, was I a fool in school for cutting gym.
                            D
  This guy's got 'em scared to death.
B7/D♯                          Em
Hope he doesn't see right through me.
D/F♯                       G              C
Now I really wish that I knew how to swim.
```

Chorus 3

```
     D       C/E              D/F♯
(Be  a  man!)  We must be swift as the coursing river,
     G        C                D              B7/D♯          Em
(Be a man!)  With all the force of a great    typhoon,
              C                D              B7/D♯          Em
(Be a man!)   With all the strength of a rag - ing fire
       C                 D                   Em
Mys-te-ri-ous as the dark  side of the moon.
```

Verse 3

```
Fm        E♭/G   A♭
   Time is racing t'ward us
         B♭m    E♭
'Til   the Huns ar-rive.
Fm          E♭/G  A♭
   Heed my ev'ry order
         B♭m       E♭/G
And you might sur-vive.
```

```
                 D♭/F              E♭/G
Chorus 4     You're un-suit-ed for the rage of war.
                 A♭                          D♭
             So pack up, go home, you're through.
                                E♭            Fm         Fsus4
             How could I make a man out of you?

                 D♭/F              E♭/G
Chorus 5     (Be a man!)  We must be swift as the coursing river,
                A♭          D♭               E♭                  C/E            Fm
             (Be a man!)  With all the force of a great     typhoon,
                          D♭              E♭                    C/E     Fm
             (Be a man!)   With all the strength of a rag - ing fire
                   D♭                 E♭                           Fm
             Mys-te-ri-ous as the dark side of the moon.

                 D♭/F N.C.
Outro        (Be a man!)     We must be swift as the coursing river,

             (Be a man!) With all the force of a great typhoon,

             (Be a man!) With all the strength of a raging fire,
                   D♭                 E♭add9                        Fm
             Mys-te-ri-ous as the dark side of the moon.
```

Into the Unknown

from FROZEN 2

Music and Lyrics by Kristen Anderson-Lopez and Robert Lopez

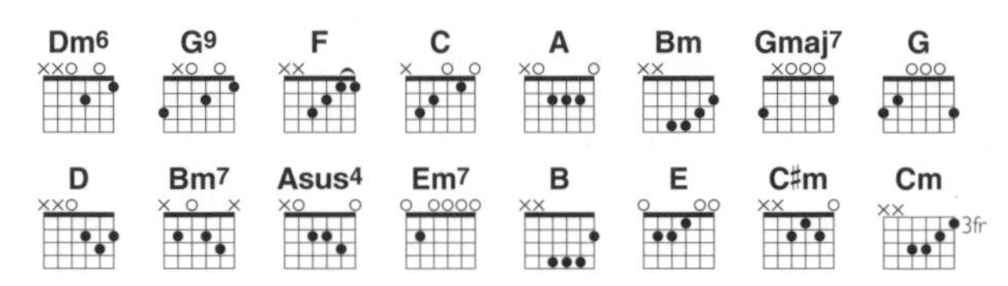

To match original recording, place capo on 1st fret

Intro

| Dm6 | | G9 | | |
(Ah.)

| Dm6 | | G9 | | |
(Ah.) (Ah.)

Verse 1

Dm6
I can hear you, but I won't.
G9
Some look for trouble, while others don't.
F C
There's a thousand reasons I should go about my day
F C
And ig-nore your whispers, which I wish would go away...
Dm6 G9
Oh. (Ah. Oh. Ah.)

Verse 2

Dm6
You're not a voice, you're just a ringing in my ear,
G9
And if I heard you, which I don't,

I'm spoken for, I fear.
F C
Ev'ryone I've ever loved is here within these walls.
G9 A
I'm sorry, secret siren, but I'm blocking out your calls.

Pre-Chorus

Bm
I've had my adventure. I don't need something new!
Gmaj7 G
I'm a-fraid of what I'm risking if I follow you

Chorus

```
                   D                          G
Into the unknown... Into the unknown... Into the unknown!
Bm7   G
     (Ah. Ah.)
```

Verse 3

```
               Dm6
What do you want? 'Cause you've been keeping me awake.
            G9
Are you here to distract me so I make a big mistake?
N.C.               F                          C
     Or are you someone out there who's a little bit like me?
     G                        Asus4                  N.C.
Who knows deep down I'm not where I'm meant to be?
```

Pre-Chorus

```
        Bm
Ev'ry day's a little harder as I feel my power grow!
Gmaj7                   G               Em7          N.C.
Don't you know there's part of me that longs to go...
```

Chorus

```
Gmaj7              D                         G
Into the unknown?  Into the unknown!   Into the unknown!
Bm7  G
       (Ah. Ah.)
```

Bridge

```
                A
Oh, are you out there? Do you know me?
          G
Can you feel me? Can you show me?
```

Interlude

```
      B    E    B       E
(Ah,  ah,  ah,  ah,  ah,  ah.)
```

Outro

```
C#m                                       A
Where are you going? Don't leave me a-lone!
C         Cm
How do I follow you
N.C.            B
      Into the un-known?
```

I'm Late

from ALICE IN WONDERLAND

Words by Bob Hilliard
Music by Sammy Fain

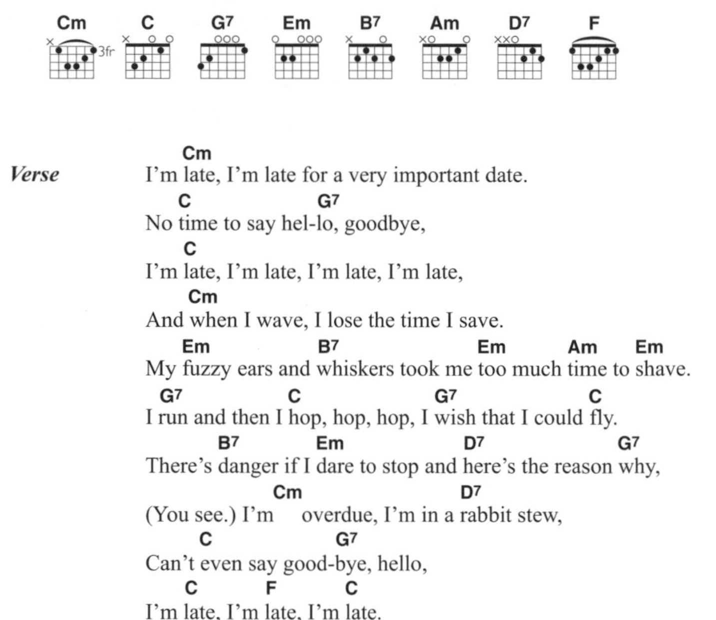

It's a Small World

from Disney Parks' "It's a Small World" Attraction

Words and Music by Richard M. Sherman
and Robert B. Sherman

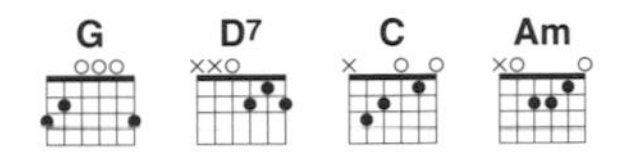

Verse

```
         G                         D7
It's a world of laughter, a world of tears.
                                  G
It's a world of hopes and a world of fears.

There's so much that we share
           C               Am
That it's time we're a-ware.
     D7                   G
It's a small world after all.
                       D7
It's a small world after all.
                       G
It's a small world after all.
                       C      Am
It's a small world after all.
     D7              G
It's a small, small world.
                                         D7
There is just one moon and one golden sun,
                                        G
And a smile means friendship to ev'ryone.
                                                  C              Am
Though the mountains divide and the oceans are wide,
     D7                   G
It's a small world after all.
```

Kiss the Girl

from THE LITTLE MERMAID

Music by Alan Menken
Lyrics by Howard Ashman

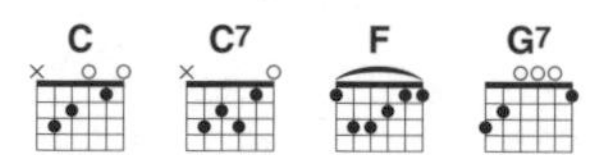

Verse 1

```
C                                                    C7
   There you see her sitting there across the way.
F                                                    C
She don't got a lot to say, but there's something a-bout her.
          G7
And you don't know why, but you're dying to try.
             C
You wanna    kiss the girl.
                                                      C7
Yes, you want her. Look at her, you know you do.
F                                                    C
Possible she wants you, too. There is one way to ask her.
         G7
It don't take a word, not a single word,
            C
Go on and   kiss the girl.
```

Chorus 1

```
C                          F
   Sha, la, la, la, la, la, my oh my.
                C
Look like the boy too shy.
              G7
Ain't gonna    kiss the girl.
C                          F
   Sha, la, la, la, la, la, ain't that sad.
          G7
Ain't it a shame, too bad.
            C
He gonna    miss the girl.
```

Verse 2

```
C                                            C7
Now's your moment, floating in a blue lagoon.
F                                        C
Boy, you better do it soon, no time will be better.
          G7
She don't say a word and she won't say a word
          C
Until you   kiss the girl.
```

Chorus 2

```
C                     F
  Sha, la, la, la, la, la, don't be scared.
            C                        G7
You got the mood prepared, go on and   kiss the girl.
C                     F
  Sha, la, la, la, la, la, don't stop now.
            G7                    C
Don't try to hide it how you wanna   kiss the girl.
                   F
Sha, la, la, la, la, la, floating along.
          C                       G7
And listen to the song, the song say   kiss the girl.
C                        F
  Sha, la, la, la, la, la, the music play.
            G7                   C
Do what the music say. You gotta   kiss the girl.
```

Outro

```
C
You've got to kiss the girl. You wanna kiss the girl.

You've gotta kiss the girl. Go on and kiss the girl.
```

Just Around the Riverbend

from POCAHONTAS

Music by Alan Menken
Lyrics by Stephen Schwartz

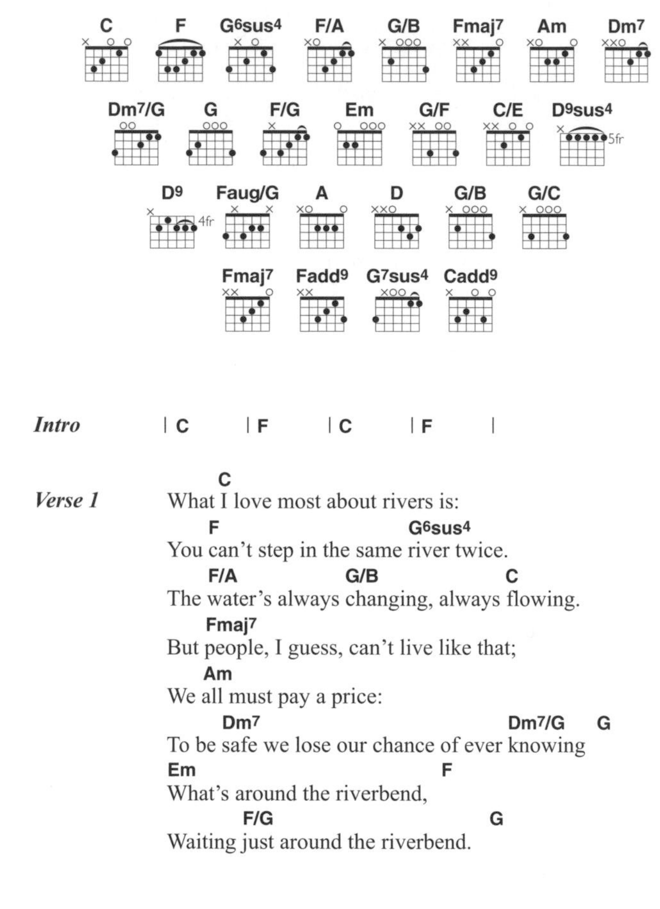

Chorus 1

```
 G/F  C/E  F
I look once more
C
Just around the riverbend
    G/F   C/E F
Be-yond the  shore,
C
Where the gulls fly free.
        Am
Don't know what for,
D9sus4               D9
What I dream the day might send
F/G                 Faug/G     G
Just around the riverbend
A         D
For me,
                         A    D
Coming for me.
```

Verse 2

```
  C
I feel it there beyond those trees
    F                         G6sus4
Or right behind these waterfalls.
      F/A          G/B                 C
Can I ignore the sound of distant drumming
       Fmaj7
For a handsome sturdy husband
               G/A                Am
Who builds handsome sturdy walls
      Dm7                                         Dm7/G    G
And never dreams that something might be coming
Em                               F
Just around the riverbend?
F/G                              G
Just around the riverbend...
```

Chorus 2

```
G   G/F  C/E  F
I   look once more
C
Just around the riverbend
   G/F  C/E F
Be-yond the  shore,
C
Somewhere past the sea.
       Am
Don't know what for...
D9sus4          D9
Why do all my dreams extend
F/G                         Faug/G
Just around the riverbend?
Dm7/G
Just around the riverbend.
```

Bridge

```
Fadd9
Should I choose the smoothest course,
C/E                      Fadd9
Steady as the beating drum?
F/A                       G/B
Should I marry Ko-co-um?
  C                           Fadd9
Is all my dreaming at an end?
Am
Or do you still wait for me, Dream Giver,
Dm7               G7sus4  C       F  Cadd9
Just around the river  -  bend?
```

Lava

from LAVA

Music and Lyrics by James Ford Murphy

C G7 F C7

```
Intro        | C      |        | G7     |        |

             | F      |        | C      | G7     |        |


             C                               G7
Verse 1         A long, long time ago           there was a volcano,
             F                                C                 G7
                Living all alone in the middle of the sea.
             C                                 G7
             He sat high above his bay, watching all the couples play,
             F                            C                       G7
                And wishing that he had someone too.
             C                                          G7
                And from his lava came this song of hope
                               F                     C              G7
             That he sang out loud ev'ry day for years and years.


             F                           C
Chorus 1        "I have a dream I hope will come true,
             G7                                   C              C7
             You're here with me, and I'm here with you.
              F                                        C
             I wish that the earth, sea, and the sky up above
                 F          G7          C
             Will send me someone to lava."


Interlude 1  | F      |        | G7     |

             |        | G      |        |
```

```
             C                               G7
*Verse 2*    Years of singing all alone turned his lava into stone,
                 F                    C                  G7
             Un - til he was on the brink of extinct - tion.
             C                                 G7
                 But little did he know that, living in the sea below,
             F                         C                G7
             Another volcano was listening to his song.
             C                                    G7
                 Ev'ry day she heard his tune, her lava grew and grew
                 F                          C                           G7
             Be - cause she believed his song was meant for her.
             C                                G7
                 Now she was so ready to meet him above the sea
                   F                             C              G7
             As he sang his song of hope for the last time.
```

Chorus 2 — *As Chorus 1*

```
Interlude 2   | C          |          |
```

```
             C                                G7
*Verse 3*    Rising from the sea below stood a lovely volcano
             F                             C                   G7
             Looking all around, but she could not see him.
                 C                                  G7
             He tried to sing to let her know that she was not there alone
                 F                C             G7
             But with no lava his song was all gone.
                 C
             He filled the sea with his tears,
                           G7
                     and watched his dreams disappear
                 F                                C                G7
             As she remembered what his song meant to her.
```

Chorus 3 — *As Chorus 1*

```
Interlude 3    | C     |     |     |     |

               C                              G7
Verse 4        Oh, they were so happy to fin'lly meet above the sea.
               F                              C                G7
                   All together now their lava grew and grew.
                   C                                    G7
               No longer are they all alone, with a - loha as their new home.
               F                                  C                G7
                   And when you visit them this is what they sing...

               F                         C
Outro-Chorus       "I have a dream I hope will come true,
                   G7                                  C                C7
               That you'll grow old with me and I'll grow old with you.
               F                                   C
               We thank the earth, sea, and the sky we thank too.
               F  G7    C
               I  lava  you."
               F  G7    C
               I  lava  you.
               F  G7    C
               I  lava  you."
```

Let It Go

from FROZEN

Music and Lyrics by Kristen Anderson-Lopez and Robert Lopez

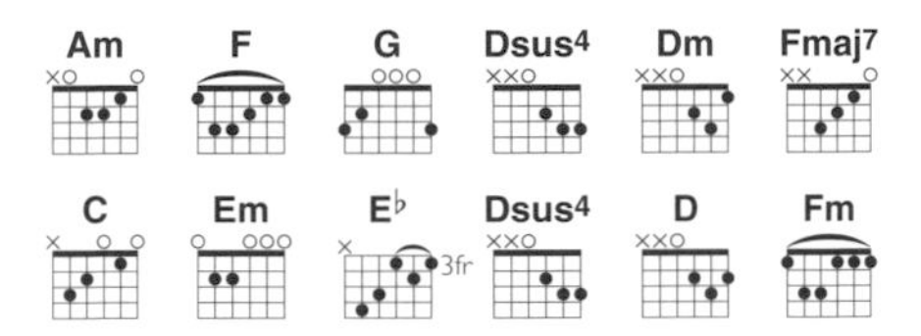

To match original recording, place capo on 8th fret

```
                 Am                                F
Verse 1          The snow glows white on the mountain tonight;
                      G                    Dsus4  Dm
                 Not a footprint to be seen.
                   Am              Fmaj7
                 A kingdom of iso-la-tion,
                      G                            Dsus4  D
                 And it looks like I'm the queen.
                 Am                Fmaj7             G                    Dsus4 Dm
                    The wind is howling like this swirling storm inside.
                 Am                         G                D
                    Couldn't keep it in;   heaven knows I   tried.

                 G
Pre-Chorus 1        Don't let them in, don't let them see.
                 F
                    Be the good girl you always have to be.
                 G                                            F
                    Conceal, don't feel, don't let them know...

                 Well, now they know.
```

Chorus 1

C G
Let it go, let it go;
Am F
Can't hold it back anymore.
C G
Let it go, let it go;
Am F
Turn away and slam the door.
C G Am F
I don't care what they're going to say:
Em E♭
Let the storm rage on.
F C G
The cold never bothered me anyway.

Verse 2

Am F
It's funny how some dis - tance
G Dm
Makes ev'rything seem small;
Am G
And the fears that once controlled me
Dsus4 D
Can't get to me at all.

Pre-Chorus 2

G
It's time to see what I can do,
F G
To test the limits and break through.
F
No right, no wrong, no rules for me;
I'm free!

Chorus 2

```
           C         G
Let it go,    let it go;
     Am                           F
I am one with the wind and sky.
           C          G
Let it go,    let it go;
       Am            F
You'll never see me cry.
C      G          Am       F
Here I stand and here I'll stay;
       Em          E♭
Let the storm rage on.
```

Bridge

```
F
    My power flurries through the air into the ground.

    My soul is spiraling in frozen fractals all around.
G
    And one thought crystallizes like an icy blast:
A              Fmaj7           G                  Dm   F
    I'm never going back; the past is in the past!
```

Chorus 3

```
           C         G
Let it go,    let it go,
             Am                       F
And I'll rise    like the break of dawn.
           C          G
Let it go,    let it go;
     Am          F
That perfect girl is gone.
C      G             Am      F     Fm
Here I stand in the light of day;
       Em          E♭
Let the storm rage on.
    F
The cold never bothered me anyway.
```

Little April Shower

from BAMBI

Music and Lyrics by Frank Churchill and Larry Morey

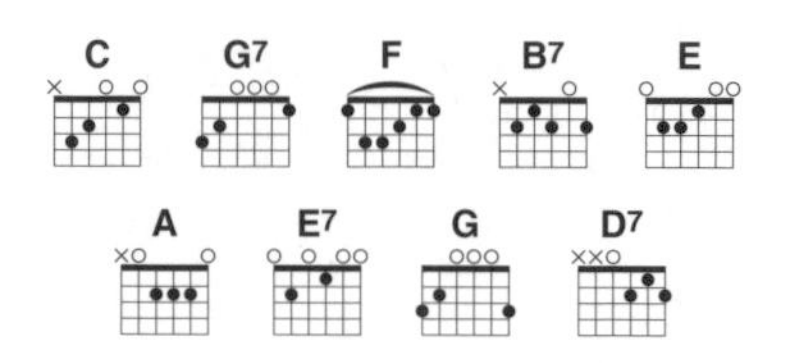

Verse 1

C G7 C F
Drip, drip, drop little April shower
C F C
Beating a tune as you fall all around
G7 C F
Drip, drip, drop little April shower
C F C
What can com-pare with your beautiful sound

Beautiful sound, beautiful sound?

Drip, drop, drip, drop

Verse 2

C G7 C F
Drip, drip, drop when the sky is cloudy
C F C
Your pretty music will brighten the day
C G7 C F
Drip, drip, drop when the sky is cloudy
C F C
You come a-long with a song right away
B7
Come with your beautiful music

Verse 3

E B7 E A
Drip, drip, drop little April shower
E E7 A E
Beating a tune as you fall all a-round
B7 E A
Drip, drip, drop little April shower
E E7 A E
What can com-pare with your beautiful sound?

```
            G         D7            G     C
Verse 4     Drip, drip, drop when the sky is cloudy
            G          C            G
            You come a-long, come a-long with your pretty little song
                      D7            G     C
            Drip, drip, drop when the sky is cloudy
            G          C            G
            You come a-long, come a-long with your pretty little song

            G
Bridge      Gay little roundalay, gay little roundalay

            Song of the rainy day, song of the rainy day
            G7
            How I love to hear your patter, pretty little pitter-patter

            Helter-skelter when you pelter, troubles always seem to scatter

            C         G7          C    F
Verse 5     Drip, drip, drop little April shower
            C      F          C
            Beating a tune as you fall all around
                      G7          C    F
            Drip, drip, drop little April shower
            C             F              C
            What can com-pare with your beautiful sound?
```

Life Is a Highway

featured in CARS

Words and Music by Tom Cochrane

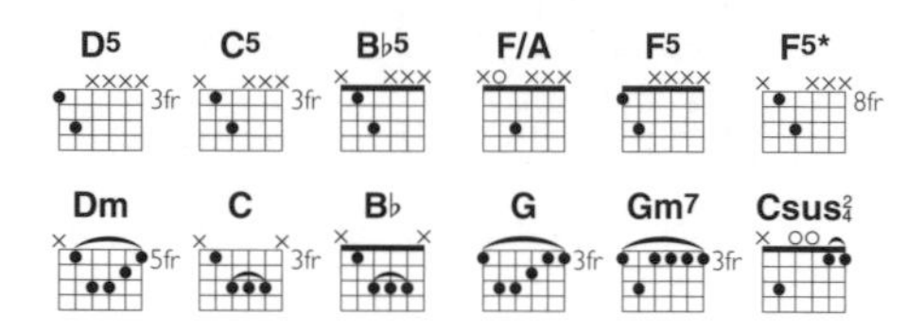

Intro

‖: N.C. | | | :‖

| D5 C5 | B♭5 | F/A | F5 |

| B♭5 F | C5 | B♭5 F5 | C5 |

| D5 F5* D5 C5 | B♭5 | F/A | F5 |

| B♭5 F5 | C5 | B♭5 F5 | C5 |

Verse 1

B♭5
Life's like a road that you travel on
F5
When there's one day here and the next day gone.
C5
Some-times you bend, sometimes you stand,

Sometimes you turn your back to the wind.
B♭5
There's a world outside ev'ry darkened door
F5
Where blues won't haunt you anymore.
C5
Where the brave are free and lovers soar,

Come ride with me to the distant shore.

```
               Dm                                C
Pre-Chorus 1     We won't hesitate     to break down the garden gate.
               B♭                                       G
                 There's not much time left to-day.

                   D5  C5      B♭5
Chorus 1       Life is a     high - way.
                 F/A    F5          B♭5        F5  C5    B♭5   F5   C5
               I wanna ride it all      night      long.
                 D5      F5*  D5   C5  B♭5
               If you're go - ing  my     way,
                 F/A    F5           B♭5        F5  C5    B♭5   F5    C5
               I wanna drive it all      night      long.

                          B♭5
Verse 2        Through all these cities and all these towns,
                  F5
               It's in my blood and it's all around.
                C5
               I love you now like I loved you then.

               This is the road and these are the hands.
                      B♭5
               From Mo - zambique to those Memphis nights,
                   F5
               The Khy - ber Pass to Vancouver's lights.
               C5
               Knock me down, I'm back up again,

               You're in my blood, I'm not a lonely man.
```

Pre-Chorus 2

Dm
There's no load I can't hold.
C
The road's so rough, this I know.
B♭
I'll be there when the light comes in.
G
Just tell 'em we're survivors.

Chorus 2

D5 C5 B♭5
‖: Life is a high - way.
F/A F5 B♭5 F5 C5 B♭5 F5 C5
I wanna ride it all night long.
D5 F5* D5 C5 B♭5
If you're go - ing my way,
F/A F5 B♭5 F5 C5 B♭5 F5 C5
I wanna drive it all night long. :‖

Bridge

Gm7 B♭
There was a dis - tance
Dm C
Between you and I.
Gm7 B♭
A mis-un-der-stand-ing once,
Dm Csus$^{2}_{4}$
But now we look it in the eye.

Guitar Solo *As Chorus 1 (Instrumental)*

```
                     Dm
Pre-Chorus 3  There ain't no load that I can't hold.
                   C
              The road's so rough, this I know.
              B♭
              I'll be there when the light comes in.
              G
              Tell 'em we're survivors.

              N.C.
Chorus 3      Life is a highway.

              I wanna ride it all night long.

              If you're going my way,

              I wanna drive it all night long.

              A gimme, gimme, gimme, a gimme, gimme, yeah.

                   D5 C5 B♭5
Chorus 4      Life is a   highway.
               F/A    F5       B♭5     F5 C5   B♭5   F5   C5
              I wanna ride it all   night   long.
                D5     F5*  D5  C5 B♭5
              If you're go - ing my   way,
               F/A    F5        B♭5     F5 C5
              I wanna drive it all   night   long.
                         B♭5   F/A    F5       C5
              Come on, gimme,  gim-me, gim-me,

                     Gimme, gimme, gimme, yeah.
```

Chorus 5 *As Chorus 1*

Outr-Gtr Solo *As Chorus 1 (Instrumental) and fade*

Love Is an Open Door

from FROZEN

Music and Lyrics by Kristen Anderson-Lopez
and Robert Lopez

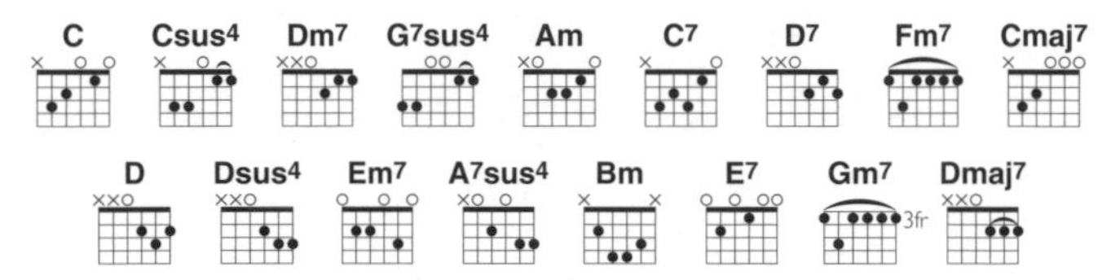

To match original recording, place capo on 2nd fret

Verse 1

C Csus4 Dm7 G7sus4
All my life has been a series of doors in my face,
C Csus4 Dm7 G7sus4
And then suddenly, I bump into you!
C Csus4 Dm7 G7sus4
I've been searching my whole life to find my own place.
C Csus4 Dm7 G7sus4
And maybe it's the party talking, or the choc'late fondue...
Am
But with you, but with you,
C
I found my I place. I see your face,
C7 D7 Fm7
And it's nothing like I've ever known be-fore.

Chorus 1

N.C. C Cmaj7 D7
Love is an open door.
Fm7 C Cmaj7 D7
Love is an open door.
Fm7
Love is an open door
C Cmaj7 D7
With you, with you, with you! With you!
Fm7 C Csus4 Dm7 G7sus4
Love is an open door.

Verse 2

```
              D
I mean it's crazy!

What?
    Dsus4                     Em7
We finish each other's... ...sandwiches!
                A7sus4
That's what I was gonna say!
D                   Dsus4                Em7
Met someone who thinks so much like me.

Jinx!
A7sus4
    Jinx again!
     D                        Dsus4
Our mental synch-ron-iz-a-tion
     Em7                      A7sus4
Can have but one ex-pla-na-tion:
D               Dsus4
You and I were just
                Em7  A7sus4
Meant to be.
                Bm
Say goodbye,
        D                   D7
To the pain of the past;
E7                                 Gm7
We don't have to feel it anymore.
```

Chorus 2

```
N.C.                D    Dmaj7   D7
Love is an open door.
Gm7                 D    Dmaj7   D7
Love is an open door.
Gm7                      D
Life can be so much more
           Dmaj7                 E7
With you,        with you, with you! With you!
Gm7                 D     Dsus4   Em7   A7sus4   D
Love is an open door.
```

Mickey Mouse March

from THE MICKEY MOUSE CLUB

Words and Music by Jimmie Dodd

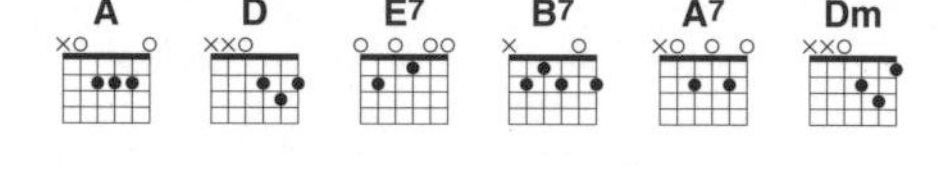


```
            N.C.
Intro       Mickey Mouse Club! Mickey Mouse Club!

            A
Verse 1     Who's the leader of the club
                     B7                   E7
            That's made for you and me?
            A        A7    D        Dm
            M - I - C  -  K - E - Y
            A        E7       A
            M - O - U - S - E!

            A
Verse 2     Hey, there! Hi, there! Ho, there!
                         B7                  E7
            You're as welcome as can be!
            A        A7    D        Dm
            M - I - C  -  K - E - Y
            A        E7       A
            M - O - U - S - E!
```

```
            D                 A
Bridge      Mickey Mouse! Mickey Mouse!
                B7                               E7
            For-ev-er let us hold our banner high!

            (High! High! High!)

            A
Verse 3     Come along and sing a song
                  B7                E7
            And join the jam-bo-ree!
            A       A7   D       Dm
            M - I - C  - K - E - Y
            A        E7     A
            M - O - U - S - E!
```

My Funny Friend and Me

from THE EMPEROR'S NEW GROOVE

Lyrics by Sting
Music by Sting and David Hartley

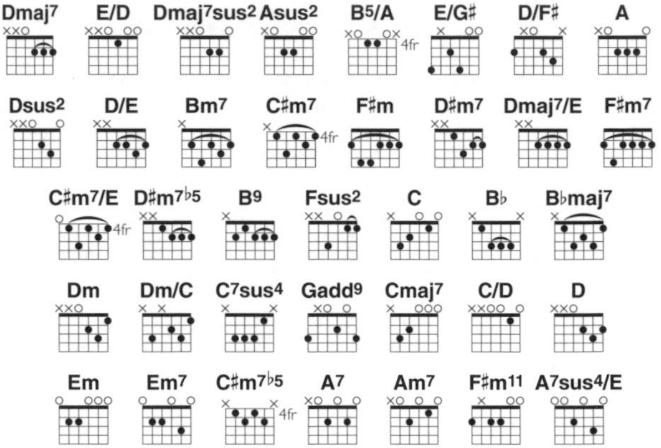

Dmaj7 E/D Dmaj7sus2 Asus2 B5/A E/G♯ D/F♯ A

Dsus2 D/E Bm7 C♯m7 F♯m D♯m7 Dmaj7/E F♯m7

C♯m7/E D♯m7♭5 B9 Fsus2 C B♭ B♭maj7

Dm Dm/C C7sus4 Gadd9 Cmaj7 C/D D

Em Em7 C♯m7♭5 A7 Am7 F♯m11 A7sus4/E

Intro ‖: Dmaj7 E/D | Dmaj7sus2 :‖

Verse 1

```
Asus2                       B5/A  E/G♯
   In the quiet time of  the   evening,
D/F♯                                A          Dsus2
   When the stars assume their patterns
Asus2                              E/G♯
   And the day has made his journey,
Dmaj7                              D/E                Dmaj7
   And we wonder just what happened to the life we knew,
              Bm7    C♯m7                    F♯m                D♯m7
Before the world changed, when not a thing I held was true.
Dmaj7                              D/E
   But you were kind to me,      and you reminded me
```

Verse 2

Asus2 B5/A E/G♯
That the world is not my playground;
D/F♯ A Dsus2
There are other things that matter;
Asus2 E/G♯
What is simple needs pro-tec-ting.
Dmaj7 D/E Dmaj7 Bm7 C♯m7
My illusions all would shatter, but you stayed in my cor - ner.
F♯m D♯m7
The only world I knew was upside down,
Dmaj7 Dmaj7/E
And now the world and me will know you carried me.
Asus2 E/G♯
You see the patterns in the big sky;
Dmaj7 E/G♯
Those constellations look like you and I.
F♯m7 C♯m7/E
Just like the patterns in the big sky,
D♯m7♭5 B9
We could be lost; we could re-fuse to try.
Dmaj7 Bm7 C♯m7
But to have made it through in the dark night,
F♯m D♯m7
Who would these lucky guys turn out to be,
Dmaj7 D/E Asus2 E/G♯
But that unusual blend of my funny friend and me.

Chorus 1

Asus2 E/G♯
You see the patterns in the big sky;
Dmaj7 E/G♯
Those constellations look like you and I.
F♯m7 C♯m7/E
Just like the patterns in the big sky,
D♯m7♭5 B9
We could be lost; we could refuse to try.
Dmaj7 Bm7 C♯m7
But to have made it through in the dark night,
F♯m D♯m7
Who would these lucky guys turn out to be,
Dmaj7 D/E Asus2 E/G♯
But that unusual blend of my funny friend and me.

Verse 3

Asus2 B5/A E/G♯
I'm not as clever as I thought I was.
D/F♯ A Dsus2
I'm not the boy I used to be, be-cause
Asus2
You showed me something diff'rent;
E/G♯
You showed me something pure.
Dmaj7 D/E
I always seemed so certain, but I was real - ly never sure.
Dmaj7 Bm7 C♯m7
But you stayed, and you called my name
F♯m D♯m7
When others would have walked out on a lou - sy game.
Dmaj7 D/E
And look who made it through
Fsus2
but your funny friend and you.

C B♭

Outro-Chorus You see the patterns in the big sky.

B♭maj7 C

Those constellations look like you and I.

Dm Dm/C

That tiny planet and the bigger guy.

B♭maj7 C7sus4

I don't know whether I should laugh or cry.

Gadd9 D/F♯

Just like the pattern in the big sky,

(We'll be together, ooh.)

Cmaj7 C/D D

We'll be together till the end of time.

Em Em7

Don't know the answer or the reason why

(We'll stick together.)

C♯m7♭5 A7

We'll stick together till the day we die.

Cmaj7 Am7 Bm7

If I have to do this all a second time,

Em7 C♯m7

I won't complain or make a fuss.

Cmaj7 C♯m7♭5

Who would the angel send, but that unlikely blend

C/D

Of these two funny friends?

Gadd9 F♯m11 A7sus4/E D Cmaj7 C/D Gadd9

That's us.

No Way Out
(Theme from BROTHER BEAR)
from BROTHER BEAR

Words and Music by Phil Collins

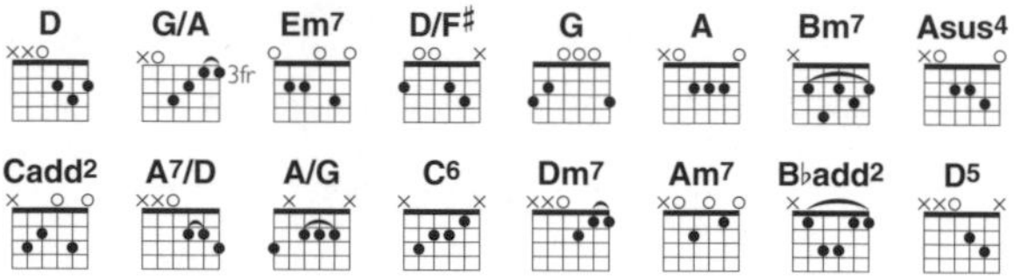

D G/A Em7 D/F♯ G A Bm7 Asus4
Cadd2 A7/D A/G C6 Dm7 Am7 B♭add2 D5

Verse 1

```
D                                   G/A
      Ev'rywhere I turn, I hurt someone,
                D
But there's nothing I can say to change
      Em7
The things I've done.
           D/F♯             G
I'd do anything with-in my pow'r;
     A                            Bm7
I'd give ev'rything I've got,
          G                                    Asus4   A
But the path I seek is hidden from me now.
```

Verse 2

```
D                            G/A
      Brother Bear, I let you down.
      D                                            Em7
You trusted me, believed in me and I let you down.
     D/F♯              G
Of all the things I hid from you,
  A                 Bm7          G
I cannot hide the shame, and I pray someone,
                                 Asus4   A        Asus4
Something will come to take a - way the pain.
```

```
            D              A          G        A
Verse 3         There's no  way out    of this  dark place.
            D            A        G     A
                No hope,   no fu-ture.
            Bm7        Em7  A           D
                I know     I     can't be free,
            Em7     Bm7            Cadd2
                But I can't see an-oth-er way,
                 Em7    Bm7     Cadd2
            And I can't face an-oth-er day.
```

```
Outro       | A7/D    | D        | A/G  G | D        |

            | A/G     | D        | A/G  G | D        |

            | C6      |          | Dm7    | Am7      |

            | B♭add2  |          | D5     |
```

Once Upon a Dream

from SLEEPING BEAUTY

Words and Music by Sammy Fain and Jack Lawrence
Adapted from a theme by Tchaikovsky

G D7 G♯dim7 Am7 B♭dim7 E7 Am D7sus4

Verse

```
G
I know you,
                         D7        G♯dim7   Am7    D7
I walked with you once up - on    a     dream.
G  B♭dim7 Am7
I   know   you,
    D7            G
The gleam in your eyes
  E7    Am7    D7
Is so fa - mi-liar a gleam.
       G
Yet, I know it's true,
                    Am7    E7      Am
That visions are seldom all they seem.
B♭dim7 G      E7
But if  I know you,
  Am7              B♭dim7
I know what you'll do;
       G             G♯dim7    E7
You'll love me at once, the way you did
Am7       D7sus4  D7    G
Once up - on        a     dream.
```

Part of Your World

from THE LITTLE MERMAID

Music by Alan Menken
Lyrics by Howard Ashman

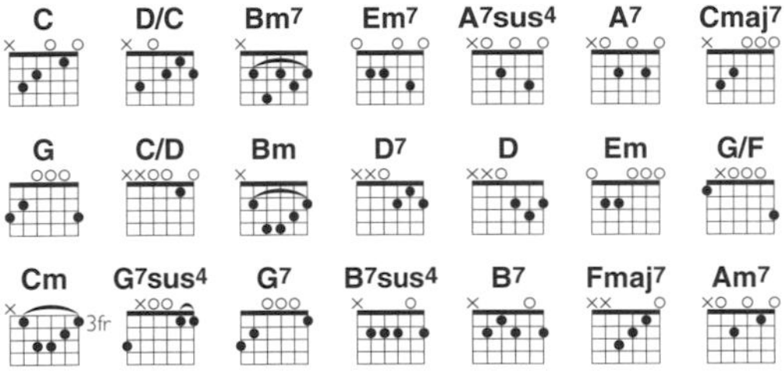

C D/C Bm7 Em7 A7sus4 A7 Cmaj7

G C/D Bm D7 D Em G/F

Cm (3fr) G7sus4 G7 B7sus4 B7 Fmaj7 Am7

Verse

```
C                          D/C
Look at this stuff. Isn't it neat?
C                                         D/C
Wouldn't you think my col-lec-tion's complete?
Bm7                                      Em7
Wouldn't you think I'm the girl,
                   A7sus4       A7
The girl who has       ev-'ry-thing.
C                          D/C
Look at this trove, treasures untold.
C                                   D/C
How many wonders can one cavern hold?
Bm7                                      Em7
Looking around here you'd think
     A7sus4                  A7
Sure,      she's got ev-'ry-thing.
```

```
              Cmaj7                  Bm7    G
Pre-Chorus  I've got gadgets and gizmos a-plenty.
              Em7                        A7sus4   A7
            I've got who-zits and what-zits ga-lore.
                Cmaj7                      Bm7     G
            You want thing-a-ma-bobs, I've got twenty.
               Em7           A7sus4   A7
            But who cares? No big deal.
                 C/D   Bm   C/D   D7
            I want more.

            G                      Bm7
Chorus      I wanna be where the people are.
            C                      C/D     D
            I wanna see, wanna see 'em dancin',
            Em                         Bm                C/D          D   D7
            Walkin' around on those,   what-d'-ya call 'em, oh, feet.
            G                            Bm
            Flippin' your fins you don't get too far.
            C                        C/D      D
            Legs are required for jumpin', dancin'.
            Em                         Bm            C/D            D         D7
            Strollin' along down the,   what's the word again,   street.
                            G                      G/F
            Up where they walk, up where they run,
                            C                    Cm
            Up where they stay all day in the sun.
                      G                D             G
            Wanderin' free, wish I could be part of that world.
```

Bridge

```
               C               D/C             Bm
What would I give if I could live outta these waters.
Em                C                D/C             Bm
   What would I pay to spend a day warm on the sand?
G7sus4  G7         C                    D/C
            Betcha on land they un-der-stand.
                B7sus4    B7            Em
Bet they don't reprimand    their daugh - ters.
Em7              A7sus4  A7           A7sus4
   Bright young women,     sick of swimmin',
A7          Fmaj7  C/D  D  C/D
Ready to stand.
```

Outro

```
      G
And ready to know what the people know.
Cmaj7                          D7
Ask 'em my questions and get some answers.
Em                  Bm           G                Am7
What's a fire, and why does it, what's the word,     burn?
D7              G
   When's it my turn?
            G/F              C                  Cm
Wouldn't I love, love to ex-plore that shore up a-bove,
N.C.       G
Out of the sea.
                D7               C        G
Wish I could be part of that world.
```

A Pirate's Life

from PETER PAN

Words by Ed Penner
Music by Oliver Wallace

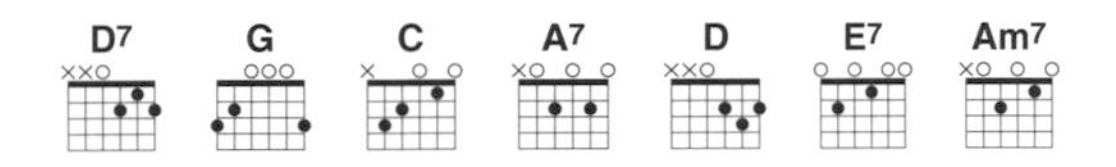

Verse 1

D7 G C G
Oh! A pirate's life is a wonderful life,
A7 D
A-roving over the sea.
E7 Am7 D7
Give me a career as buc-ca-neer,
G D7 G
It's the life of a pirate for me!
D7 G D7 G
Oh! The life of a pirate for me!

Verse 2

D7 G C G
Oh! A pirate's life is a wonderful life,
A7 D
They never bury your bones
E7 Am7 D7
For when it's all over, a jolly sea rover
G D7 G
Drops in on his friend Davy Jones
D7 G D7 G
Oh! His very good friend Davy Jones.

The Place Where Lost Things Go

from MARY POPPINS RETURNS

Music by Marc Shaiman
Lyrics by Scott Wittman and Marc Shaiman

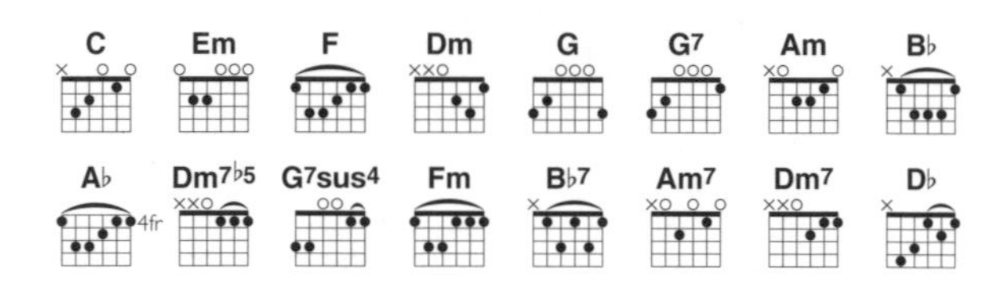

Verse 1

```
C                 Em   F          C
Do you ever lie a-wake at night,
Dm                                   G
Just between the dark and the morning light,
C                          Em          F       C
Searching for the things you used to know,
Dm                                          G7         C
Looking for the place where the lost things go?
```

Verse 2

```
                  Em         F        C
Do you ever dream or rem-in-isce,
Dm                                         G
Wond'ring where to find what you truly miss?
      C                    Em          F          C
Well, maybe all those things that you love so
   Dm                                          G7         C
Are waiting in the place where the lost things go.
```

Bridge

```
Em                   F        Em                     F
Memories you've shared, gone for good, you feared,
           Dm                Am                      B♭     G
They're all around you still, though they've   dis-ap-peared.
Em                 F        Em              A♭
Nothing's really left, or lost without a trace.
Dm7♭5                             G7sus4  G7
Nothing's gone forever, only out   of  place.
```

Verse 3

```
    C                  Em      F       C
So maybe now the dish and my best spoon
     Dm                               G
Are playing hide and seek just be-hind the moon,
C                Em    F       A♭
Waiting there un-til it's time to show.
Fm                B♭7   C              B♭7
Spring is like that now, far beneath the snow,
C            Am7                 Dm7 G7    C   Em
Hiding in the place where the lost  things go.
```

Instru

```
| F   C  | Dm     | G7  C  |        |
```

Bridge

```
Em                     F      Em                F
Time to close your eyes so sleep can come a-round,
     Dm                          Am          B♭     G
For when you dream, you'll find all that's lost is found.
Em            F          Em                  A♭
Maybe on the moon, or maybe somewhere new,
Dm7♭5                                  G7sus4   G7
Maybe all you're missing lives in-side   of   you.
```

Verse 4

```
     C                   Em         F       C
So, when you need her touch and loving gaze,
Dm                                G
"Gone, but not forgotten," is the perfect phrase.
C               Em       F          A♭
Smiling from a star that she makes glow,
Fm                  B♭7    C               B♭7
Trust she's always there, watching as you grow.
C              Am7                Dm7 G7     A♭  D♭  A♭  C
Find her in the place where the lost  things go.
```

Reflection

from MULAN

Music by Matthew Wilder
Lyrics by David Zippel

E C♯m11 F♯m B7 D7 Gadd9 Em7

Am7 Cm6/9 G D/C C D/F♯ Em

Cmaj7 C6 F D D7sus4 Bm7 C♯m7♭5

Verse 1

E C♯m11 F♯m
Look at me, you may think you see who I really am,
E B7
But you'll never know me.
E C♯m11 D7
Ev'ry day it's as if I play a part.
Gadd9 Em7 Am7
Now I see if I wear a mask I can fool the world,
Cm6/9 G
But I cannot fool my heart.

Chorus 1

G Em7
Who is that girl I see
D/C C Cm6/9
Staring straight back at me?
G D/F♯ Em G Cmaj7 C6
When will my re-flec-tion show
Cm6/9 G Em7
Who I am in-side?

Verse 2

E C♯m11 F♯m
I am now in a world where I have to hide my heart
B7
And what I be-lieve in.
Gadd9 Em7 Am7
But somehow I will show the world what's inside my heart,
Cm6/9 G
And be loved for who I am.

Chorus 2

G Em7
Who is that girl I see
D/C C Cm6/9
Staring straight back at me?
G D/F♯ Em G Cmaj7 C6
Why is my re - flec-tion someone
F D
I don't know?
G Em7 C Cm6/9
Must I pre-tend that I'm someone else for all time?
G D/F♯ Em G Cmaj7 Cm6/9
When will my re-flec-tion show who I am?

Pre-chorus

C Em7 Am7 D7sus4
In-side, there's a heart that must be free to fly,
Em7 Bm7 Am7 Cm6/9
That burns with a need to know the reason why.

Chorus 3

G Em7
Why must we all conceal
D/C C Cm6/9
What we think, how we feel?
G D/F♯ Em G Cmaj7 C6
Must there be a secret me
F D
I'm forced to hide?
G Em7 C Cm6/9
I won't pre-tend that I'm someone else for all time.
G D/F♯ Em G Cmaj7
When will my re-flec-tion show
Cm6/9 Em Em7 C♯m7♭5
Who I am in-side?
G D/F♯ Em G Cmaj7 C6
When will my re - flection show
Cm6/9 G Em7 G
Who I am in-side?

Remember Me
(Ernesto de la Cruz)
from COCO

Words and Music by Kristen Anderson-Lopez and Robert Lopez

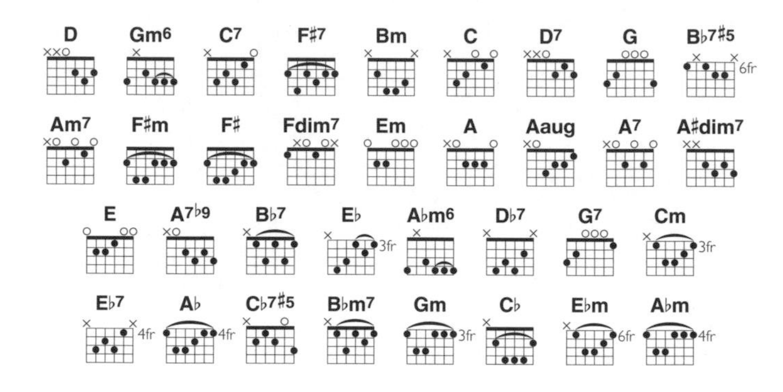

Verse 1

D Gm6
Remember me, though I have to say goodbye.
D C7 F♯7
Remember me, don't let it make you cry.
Bm C D7
For even if I'm far away, I hold you in my heart.
G B♭7♯5
I sing a secret song to you each night we are apart.
D Gm6
Remember me, though I have to travel far.
D Am7 D7
Remember me each time you hear a sad gui-tar.
G F♯m F♯ Bm Fdim7
Know that I'm with you the only way that I can be.
Em A Aaug D A
Until you're in my arms a-gain, re-mem-ber me.

Interlude

D	G A	D
G A7 A♯dim7	Bm	D7
E	A	A7♭9

Verse 2

B♭7 E♭ A♭m6
Remember me, though I have to say goodbye.
E♭ D♭7 G7
Remember me, don't let it make you cry.
Cm D♭ E♭7
For even if I'm far away, I hold you in my heart.
A♭ C♭7♯5
I sing a secret song to you each night we are apart.
E♭ A♭m6
Remember me, though I have to travel far.
E♭ B♭m7 E♭7
Remember me each time you hear a sad gui-tar.
A♭ Gm G Cm C♭
Know that I'm with you the only way that I can be.
N.C. B♭ C♭ A♭m N.C. E♭
Until you're in my arms a-gain, re-mem-ber me.

Scales and Arpeggios

from THE ARISTOCATS

Words and Music by Richard M. Sherman
and Robert B. Sherman

C G7 F F♯dim7 C/G Dm G7sus4

Intro

C
Do, mi, so, do, do, so, mi, do.

Verse 1

G7
Ev'ry truly cultered music student knows
C
You must learn your scales and you ar-peg-gi-os.
F F♯dim7
Bring the music ringing from your chest and not your nose
C/G G7 C
While you sing your scales and your ar-peg-gi-os.

Verse 2

G7
If you're faithful to your daily practising,
C
You will find your progress is en-cou-rag-ing.
F F♯dim7
Do mi so mi do mi so mi fa la, so it goes
C/G G7 C
When you do the scales and your ar-peg-gi-os.

Instru.

| G7 | C | Dm G7 |

| C G7 | C | |

C
Interlude Do, mi, so, do, do, so, mi, do.

Do, mi, so, do, do, so, mi, do.

C G7
Verse 3 Though at first it seems as tho' it doesn't show,

C
Like a tree, ability will bloom and grow.

If you're smart, you'll learn by heart what

F F♯dim7
Ev'ry artist knows:

N.C. G7sus4 G7 C G7 C
You must sing your scales and ar-peg - gi - os.

The Second Star to the Right

from PETER PAN

Words by Sammy Cahn
Music by Sammy Fain

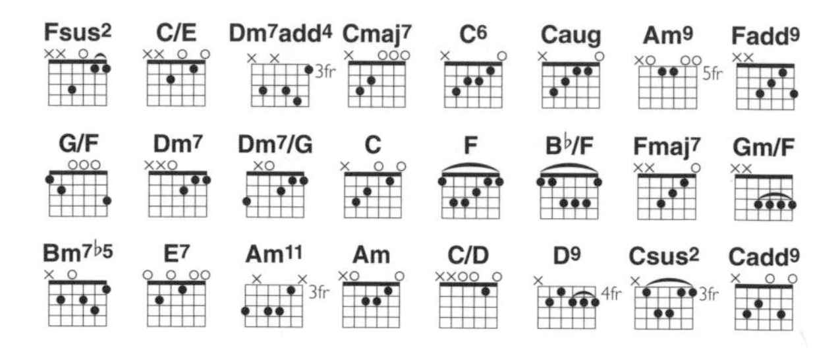

Verse 1

N.C.
The second star to the right

Shines in the night for you,
Fsus2 C/E
To tell you that the dreams you plan
Dm7add4 Cmaj7 C6
Really can come true.
Cmaj7 C6
The second star to the right
Caug Am9
Shines with a light that's rare;
Fadd9 G/F C/E
And if it's Nev-er-land you need,
Dm7 Dm/G C
Its light will lead you there.

Verse 2

F   B♭/F
Twinkle, twinkle, little star,
Fmaj7   Gm/F
So I'll know where you are.
F   Bm7♭5 E7
Gleaming in the skies a-bove,
Am11 Am C/D D9   Dm7/G
Lead me to   the land I dream of.
Cmaj7   C6
     And when our journey is through,
Caug   Am9
Each time we say good-night,
Fadd9   G/F   C/E   Am9
      I'll thank the little star that shines,
     Dm7   Dm7/G   Cmaj7
The second from the right.

Outro

| C6 | Cmaj7 | C6 |

| Csus2 | Cadd9 C |

Shut Up and Drive

featured in WRECK-IT RALPH

Words and Music by Evan Rogers, Carl Sturken, Gillian Gilbert,
Peter Hook, Stephen Morris and Bernard Sumner

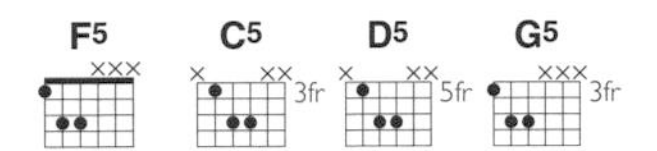

Intro

| F5 C5 | D5 | G5 C5 | D5 |

| F5 C5 | D5 | G5 C5 | D5 |

Verse 1

```
               F5                  C5                  D5
I've been looking for a driver who is qualified,
              G5                              C5              D5
So if you think that you're the one, step in-to my ride.
          F5               C5              D5
I'm a fine-tuned supersonic speed machine
            G5            C5              D5
With a sun-roof top and a gangsta lean.
```

Bridge 1

```
F5                  C5                     D5
      So if ya feel me, let me know, know, know.
G5                           C5                         D5
      Come on now, whatcha waiting for, for, for?
F5                           C5              D5
      My engine's ready to ex-plode, explode, explode.
G5                    C5                          D5
      So start me up and watch me go, go, go!
```

Chorus 1

```
               F5                     C5       D5
I'll getcha where you wanna go, if ya know what I mean.
        G5          C5                D5
Got a ride that's smoother than a limousine.
            F5                  C5          D5
Can you handle the curves,   can you run all the lights?
        G5         C5                 D5
If you can, baby boy, then we can go all night.
             F5       C5        D5
'Cause I'm zero to sixty in three point five.
        G5            C5    D5
Baby, you got the keys,
N.C.                              F5 C5 D5                       G5 C5 D5
   Now shut up and drive,              shut up and drive.
```

Verse 2

```
            F5          C5           D5
I've got class like a fifty-seven Cadillac.
               G5          C5            D5
Got all the drive, but a whole lot of boom in back.
    F5                   C5             D5
You look like you can handle what's under my hood.
             G5                 C5        D5
You keep saying that you will, boy, I wish you would.
```

Bridge 2 *As Bridge 1*

Chorus 2 *As Chorus 1*

Verse 3

N.C.
'Cause today they ain't got what I got.

Get it, get it, don't stop, it's a sure shot.

Ain't no Ferrari, huh, boy? I'm sorry.

I ain't even worried, so step inside and ride.

Interlude | F5 C5 | D5 | G5 C5 | D5 |

Bridge 3 *As Bridge 1*

Chorus 3 *As Chorus 1*

Outro

D5 F5 C5 D5 G5 C5
Shut up and drive, shut up and drive.

| D5 | F5 C5 | D5 | G5 C5 | D5 |

Someday

from THE HUNCHBACK OF NOTRE DAME

Music by Alan Menken
Lyrics by Stephen Schwartz

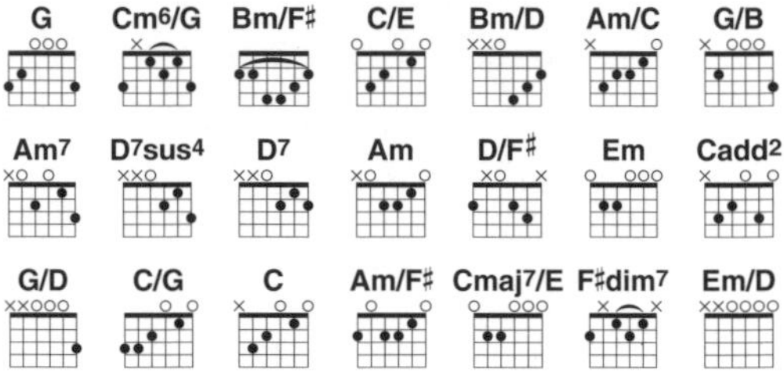

G Cm6/G Bm/F♯ C/E Bm/D Am/C G/B

Am7 D7sus4 D7 Am D/F♯ Em Cadd2

G/D C/G C Am/F♯ Cmaj7/E F♯dim7 Em/D

Intro | G Cm6/G | G Cm6/G |

Verse 1

```
G             Bm/F♯                  C/E      Bm/D
Someday            when we are wiser,
                                  Am/C     G/B
When the world's older,
                             Am7       D7sus4        D7
When we have learned,
Am      D/F♯
I pray          someday we may
Em Bm/D  Cadd2  G/B  G/D  D7sus4   D7
Yet live to live       and  let    live.
G              Bm/F♯                C/E     Bm/D
Someday          life will be fairer,
                        Am/C   G/B                          Am7    D7sus4    D7
Need will be rarer,           greed will not pay.
Am7            D/F♯                        C/G  G    C    Am/F♯  Em    Am
God speed         this bright mil - len - ni - um on          its    way.
C   D7sus4  D7      G        Bm/F♯
Let it come some-day.
```

```
Instru      | C/E    Bm/D  | Am/C    G/B  | D7sus4  D7    |

            G          Bm/F#                    C/E         Bm/D
Verse 2     Someday       our fight will be won then,
                                 Am/C       G/B
            We'll stand in the sun then,
                                 Am7       D7sus4      D7
            That bright af-ter-noon.
            Am       D/F#                      C/G    G   Cadd2
            Till then,    on days when the sun    is   gone,
            Am/F#  Em    Am        C   Cmaj7/E  F#dim7  Em       Em/D
            We'll   hang on,  wish up-on         the      moon.
            Am      G/B  Cadd2  C    D7sus4     D7  G       Cm6/G
            Change will  come   one  day, some-day soon.

Outro       | G    Cm6/G | G    Cm6/G  | G            |
```

A Spoonful of Sugar

from MARY POPPINS

Words and Music by Richard M. Sherman
and Robert B. Sherman

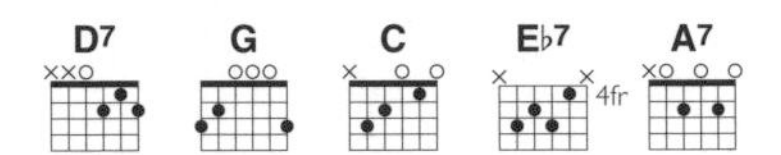

Verse 1

```
               G
In ev'ry job that must be done

There is an element of fun.
                                              D7
You find the fun and snap the job's a game.
              C                    E♭7
And ev'ry task you un-der-take
  G                      A7
Be-comes a piece of cake,
  G       D7
A lark! A spree!
   A7          D7
It's very clear to see
```

Chorus 1

```
A7    D7                                  G
That a spoonful of sugar helps the medicine go down,
    D7                       G
The medicine go down, medicine go down.
A7    D7                                 G
Just a spoonful of sugar helps the medicine go down
               D7   G  D7
In a most de-light-ful way.
```

Verse 2

```
               G
A robin feathering his nest

Has very little time to rest
                                          D7
While gathering his bits of twine and twig.
                     C                  E♭7
Though quite in-tent in his pur-suit
            G                 A7
He has a merry tune to toot.
     G          D7           A7                D7
He knows a song will move the job a-long.
A7
For a…
```

Chorus 2 *As Chorus 1*

Strangers Like Me

from TARZAN®

Words and Music by Phil Collins

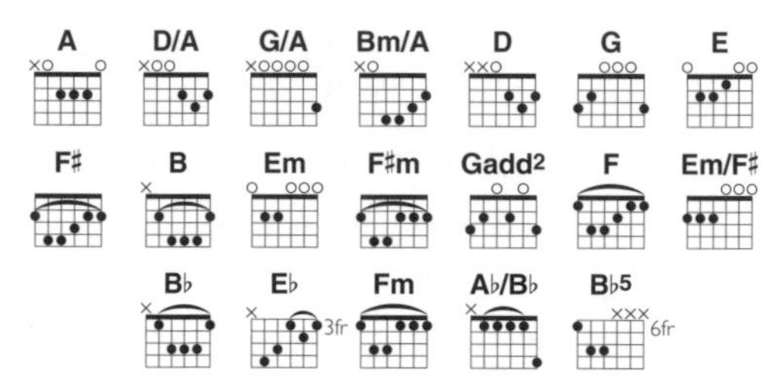

To match original recording, place capo on 1st fret

Intro

| A D/A | A G/A Bm/A |

| A D/A | A G/A |

Verse 1

A D/A A G/A
Whatever you do, I'll do it too.
A D/A A G/A
Show me ev'rything and tell me how.
A D/A A G/A A D/A A G/A
It all means something and yet nothing to me.
D G
Oh, I can see there's so much to learn.
E A
It's all so close and yet so far.
F♯ B
I see myself as people see me.
G A
Oh, I just know there's something bigger out there.

Chorus 1

D A Em D
I wanna know, can you show me?
A D A G/D
I wanna know about these strangers like me.
A D A Em D
Tell me more, please show me.
A D A G/D
Something's fa-mi-liar 'bout these strangers like me.

Instru. | A D/A | A G/A Bm/A |

| A D/A | A G/A |

Verse 2

```
A              D/A       A         G/A
      Ev'ry gesture,     ev'ry move that she makes
A              D/A       A         G/A
Makes me feel like never be-fore.
A                D/A    A                G/A        A       D/A      A G/A
    Why do I have    this growing need to be   beside   her?
D                               G
   Oh, these emotions I never knew,
  E                                 A
Of some other world far be-yond this place,
F♯                            B
   Beyond the trees, a-bove the clouds.
   G                                A
Oh, I see before me a new ho-ri-zon.
```

Chorus 2 *As Chorus 1*

Bridge

```
F♯m                  Gadd2               F♯m
         Come with me now to see my world,
                 Em                    F♯m
Where there's beauty beyond your dreams.
          Gadd2          F
Can you feel the things I feel
        E
Right now with you?
Em/F♯          Gadd2
         Take my hand.
          Em      D/F♯    Gadd2  A
There's a world I need to know.
```

```
Instru.       | A        D/A       | A    G/A  Bm/A |

              | A        D/A       | A    G/A       |

               B♭          E♭     B♭          Fm   E♭
Chorus 3          I wanna know,     can you show me?
               B♭          E♭                 B♭        A♭/B♭
                  I wanna know about these strangers like me.
               B♭          E♭     B♭        Fm    E♭
                  Tell me more,     please show me.
               B♭                   E♭                  B♭         A♭/B♭
                  Something's fa-mi-liar 'bout these strangers like me.
                            B♭5
               I wanna know!
```

Supercalifragilisticexpialidocious

from MARY POPPINS

Words and Music by Richard M. Sherman
and Robert B. Sherman

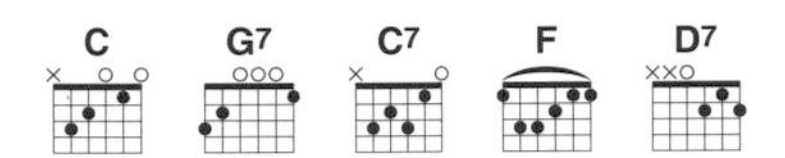

Chorus 1

```
C                                  G7
Supercalifragilisticexpiali-docious!
                                                    C
Even though the sound of it is something quite a-trocious,
                                        C7                  F
If you say it loud enough you'll always sound pre-cocious.
          C              G7        C
Supercali-fragilistic-expiali-docious!
```

Bridge

```
C                                G7
Um diddle diddle diddle, um diddle ay!
C                                G7
Um diddle diddle diddle, um diddle ay!
```

Verse

```
   C                                                   G7
Be-cause I was afraid to speak when I was just a lad,
                                                        C
Me father gave me nose a tweak and told me I was bad.
                                            C7               F
But then one day I learned a word that saved me achin' nose,
    D7                                                 G7
The biggest word you ever 'eard and this is 'ow it goes! Oh!
```

Chorus 2 *As Chorus 1*

Strong

from CINDERELLA

Words and Music by Patrick Doyle,
Kenneth Branagh and Tommy Danvers

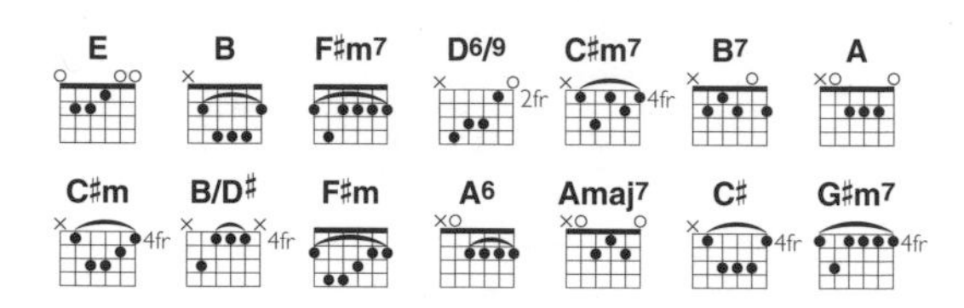

Intro | E | B | F♯m7 | D6/9 | |

Verse 1

E C♯m7 F♯m7 B7
In a perfect storybook the world is brave and good:
E C♯m7 F♯7 B7
A hero takes your hand; sweet love will fol-low.
E C♯m7 F♯m7 B7
But life's a diff'rent game, the sorrow and the pain.
E C♯m7 F♯7 B7
Only you can change your world to-mor-row.

Pre-Chorus 1

A B C♯m B/D♯ E F♯ B
Let your smile light up the sky;
A B C♯m B/D♯ E F♯ B
Keep your spi - rit soar - ing high.

Chorus 1

E B F♯m7 A
Trust in your heart, and your soul shines for-ev-er and ever.
E B F♯m7 A
Hold fast to kindness; your light shines for-ev-er and ever.
E B F♯m7 A
I believe in you and in me.
E B F♯m7 D6/9
We are strong.

Verse 2

```
           E                      C♯m7   F♯m7          B7
When once upon a time,      in stories and in rhyme,
   E                         C♯m7    F♯7          B7
A moment you can shine     and wear your own crown.
```

Pre-Chorus 2

```
A   B   C♯m B/D♯ E   F♯    B
Be  the  one  that  res-cues  you.
A          B  C♯m    B/D♯   E   F♯  B
Through the clouds you'll see the blue.
```

Chorus 2 *As Chorus 1*

Bridge

```
  A6         E           B
A bird all a-lone on the wing
    F♯m     Amaj7      B
Can still be strong and sing,
C♯
Sing.
```

Chorus 3

```
F♯              C♯                  G♯m7              B
Trust in your heart, and your soul shines for-ev-er and ever.
F♯              C♯                G♯m7              B
Hold fast to kindness; your light shines for-ev-er and ever.
F♯         C♯   G♯m7        B
I believe     in you and in me.
F♯   C♯   G♯m7    E
We  are  strong.
```

That's How You Know

from ENCHANTED

Music by Alan Menken
Lyrics by Stephen Schwartz

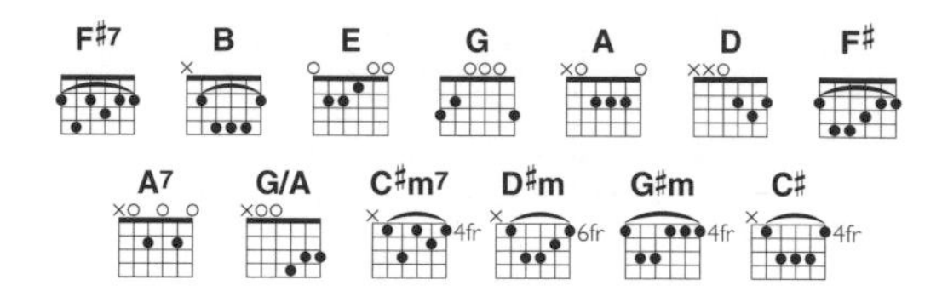

N.C.
Intro How does she know you love her?

How does she know she's yours

Chorus 1 How does she know that you love her?

How do you show her you love her?

How does she know that you really...

Really... truly... love her?

How does she know that you love her?

How do you show her you love her?

F♯7
How does she know that you real-ly,

B E G A
Really, truly love her?

Verse 1

```
D                  G
It's not enough to take the one
     A        D        G        A
You love for granted.
D
You must remind her,
G                A       F♯  B    E
Or she'll be in-clined to  say:
```

Chorus 2

```
       A7  D     G/A  D            G/A
"How do I know he    loves me?
           D      F♯7  B         E
How do I know he's mine?"
```

Verse 2

```
         F♯7      B
   Well, does he leave a little note to
E                   C♯m7           F♯7
Tell you you are on his mind?
B                            E
Send you yellow flowers when
            C♯m7        F♯7
The sky is grey? Hey.
D♯m
He'll find a new way to
G♯m                B         C♯
Show you a little bit ev'ry day.
E     F♯   E   F
That's how you know,
G     A   G   A
That's how you know
N.C.      D
He's your love.
```

Instru.

```
| G/A    | D       | G/A    | D       |

| G/A        | B     E    |       G  A |
```

Verse 3

```
D                  G          A
   (You've got to show her you need her;
D                  G          A
   Don't treat her like a mind-read-er!
D               G                F#7
   Each day do something to lead her
B    E        G   A
To be-lieve you love her.)
D                    G            A    D
Ev'rybody wants to live happily ever  after.
                  G              A
(You've got to show her you need her.)
D                    G                  F#7     B     E
Ev'rybody wants to know their true love is true.
```

Chorus 3

```
             A7      D       G/A  D      G/A
     How do you know he    loves  you?
                D      F#7  B
How do you know he's yours?
```

Verse 4

```
         E     F#7 B
Well, does he  take you out dancing
E                C#m7              F#7
Just so he can hold you close?
B                          E
Dedicate a song with words
                 C#m7           F#7
Meant just for you? Ooh.
D#m                               G#m
He'll find his own way to tell you
B                                 C#
With the little things he'll do.
E        F#    E    F#
That's how you know,
G      A    G    A      N.C.
That's how you know, he's your love.
```

Instru | D | G/A | D | G/A |

| D | G/A | B E |

Chorus 4
```
           G   A   D    G/A D        G
   That's how you know he   loves you.
     A         D     G   F♯7 B
That's how you know it's     true.
```

Verse 5
```
   E     F♯   B
Be-cause he'll wear your fav'rite color
E               C♯m7
Just so he can match your eyes;
B
Plan a private picnic
E              C♯m7        F♯7
By the fire's glow, oh.
D♯m                        G♯m
His heart'll be yours for-ev-er,
B           C♯
Something ev'ry day will show.
```

Chorus 5
```
E      F♯   E   F♯     G     A    G    A
That's how you know, that's how you know,
E      F♯   E   F♯     G     A    G    A
That's how you know, that's how you know.
```

Outro
```
E      F♯   E   F♯     G     A    G    A      N.C.
That's how you know, that's how you know,  he's your love.
                                D  G  D  A  D  G
That's how you know,
       A7        D     G  D  A  D  G
That's how you know
     A7         D   G   A  G/A   D
He's your  love.
```

This Is Me

from CAMP ROCK

Words and Music by Adam Watts and Andy Dodd

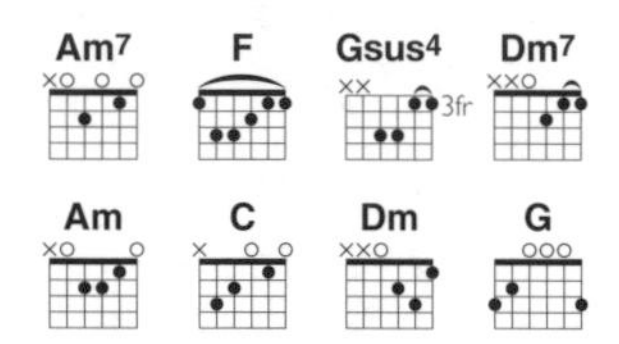

To match original recording, place capo on 1st fret

Intro | Am7 F | Gsus4 Dm7 |

Verse 1

Am7 F Gsus4 Dm7
I've always been the kind of girl that hid my face,
Am7 F Gsus4 Dm7
So a-fraid to tell the world what I've got to say.
Am F C Dm
But I have this dream bright inside of me,
Am F C Dm F
I'm gonna let it show. It's time to let you know,
G
To let you know.

Chorus 1

F C
This is real, this is me,
G Am
I'm ex-act-ly where I'm sup-posed to be, now.
F C G
Gonna let the light shine on me.
Am F C G
Now I've found who I am, there's no way to hold it in.
Dm7 F
No more hiding who I want to be,
G Am7 F
This is me.

```
              C    G            Am            F
Verse 2                 Do you know what it's like
               C            Dm
              To feel so in the dark,
                Am          F          C                  Dm
              To dream about a life where you're the shining star?
                   Am       F          C            Dm
              Even though it seems like it's too far a-way.
               Am        F          C
              I have to be-lieve in my-self.
                      Dm F
              It's the only way.

                      F       C
Chorus 2      This is real, this is me,
                      G                    Am
              I'm ex-act-ly where I'm sup-posed to be, now.
              F                        C  G
                 Gonna let the light      shine on me.
                         Am          F               C            G
              Now I've found who I am,  there's no way to hold it in.
              Dm7                                 F
              No more hiding who I want to be,
              G           Am  F  C  Dm  Am  F
                 This is me.

              G                    F          C
Bridge           You're the voice     I hear in-side my head,
                  G
              The reason that I'm singing.
                             F      C            G         Am7
              I need to find    you,    I've got to find you.
              F                       C              G
              You're the missing piece I need, the song inside of me.
              Am7      Dm                     G
              I need to find you. I've got to find you.
```

Chorus 3

```
            F          C
This is real, this is me,
         G                           Am
I'm ex-act-ly where I'm sup-posed to be, now.
F                           C G
   Gonna let the light      shine on me.
             Am           F              C                G
Now I've found who I am, there's no way to hold it in.
Dm7                                       F  G
No more hiding who I want to be,          this is me.
```

Outro

```
F                         C
You're the missing piece I need,
           Gsus4          G
The song         inside of me.
              F                C
You're the voice I hear in-side my head,
      Gsus4               Am
The reason that I'm singing.
             F            C                G
Now I've found who I am, there's no way to hold it in.
Dm7                                   F  G          F  C  G  Am  F
No more hiding who I want to be,      this is me.
```

Touch the Sky

from BRAVE

Music by Alexander L. Mandel
Lyrics by Alexander L. Mandel and Mark Andrews

D Csus4/D C/D A G Bm Bm7 Bm7add4

Play 3 times

Intro ‖: D | | | :‖

| | | |

| | | |

| | | | ‖

| | | | Csus4/D |

| D | | | C/D |

| D | | | |

| | | | |

```
             D              G
Verse 1  When cold wind is a' calling,
                D               G
         And the sky is clear and bright,
                 Bm        A      G
         Misty mountains sing and beckon,
                  D        A
         Lead me out into the light.
```

Chorus 1

Bm7 G
I will ride, I will fly,
D A Bm7
Chase the wind and touch the sky;
G
I will fly,
D A D
Chase the wind and touch the sky.

Bridge 1

G
Na, na, na, na, na, na,
D A
Na, na, na, na, na, na, na.
D G
Na, na, na, na, na, na, na, na,
D A
Na, na, na, na, na, na, na.

Instru

| Bm7add4 | | | |

| | | G |

Verse 2

D G
Where dark woods hide secrets,
D G
And mountains are fierce and bold,
Bm A G D A
Deep waters hold re-flec-tions of times lost long a-go.
D G D G
I will hear their ev'ry story, take hold of my own dream,
Bm A G
Be as strong as the seas are stormy
A D
And proud as an eagle's scream.

Chorus 2 *As Chorus 1*

Bridge 2 *As Bridge 1*

Outro

```
                    D       G       D       A       D
And touch the sky,
              G
Chase the wind,
              D      A
Chase the wind,
              D       G       D       A
Touch the sky.

| D       |       | G       |       |
| D       |       | G       |
|       | D       |       |
| G       |       | D       |
```

True Love's Kiss

from ENCHANTED

Music by Alan Menken
Lyrics by Stephen Schwartz

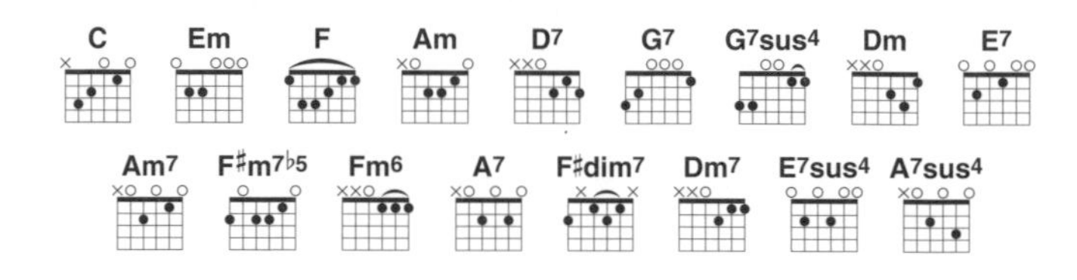

Verse 1

C Em F C
I've been dreaming of a true love's kiss;
F Am D7 G7
And a prince I'm hoping comes with this.
F C Am D7 G7sus4 G7
That's what brings ev-er-af-ter-ings so happy.
C Em F C
And that's the reason we need lips so much,
F Am Dm E7
For lips are the only things that touch.
Am Am7 F♯m7♭5 Fm6 C
So, to spend a life of endless bliss,
A7 Dm F G7 C
Just find who you love through true love's kiss.

Interude

| C Em | F C | F Am | D7 G7 |

C F♯dim7 Dm7 G7
Ah, ah, ah.
C F♯dim7 Dm7 G7
Ah, ah, ah.

Verse 2

```
C              Em                  F             C
She's been dreaming of a true love's kiss;
F     G7 Am                         D7              G7
And a   prince she's hoping comes with this.
F              Em               Am    D7        G7sus4
That's what brings ev-er-af-ter-ings so happy.
G7           C             Em                 F        C
       And that's the reason we need lips so much,
F    G7   Am            D7             E7sus4  E7
For lips are the only things that touch.
```

Outro

```
Am     Am7       F♯m7♭5  Fm6      C
So, to spend a life of   endless bliss,
A7sus4      A7          Dm7                    G7sus4  G7     C
        Just find who you love through true       love's kiss.
```

Try Everything

from ZOOTOPIA

Words and Music by Sia Furler,
Tor Erik Hermansen and Mikkel Eriksen

To match recording, place capo on 1st fret

```
             C                 F
Intro        Oh, oh, oh, oh, oh.
             C                 Gsus4
             Oh, oh, oh, oh, oh.
             C                 F
             Oh, oh, oh, oh, oh.
             C        G        C
             Oh, oh, oh, oh, oh.


Verse 1      I messed up tonight.
                         F
             I lost an-oth-er fight.
                               C                   G
             Lost to myself, but I'll just start again.
                                 C
             I keep falling down;
                              F
             I keep on hitting   the ground.
                                 C          G               C
             But I always get up,   now, to see what's next.


                                 F
Pre-Chorus 1 Birds don't just fly,
                              C          G
             They fall down    and get up.
             C                F            C G             C
             Nobody learns    without get  -  ting it wrong.
```

```
                          C                          F
Chorus 1    I won't give up; no, I won't give in
                                   C
            Till I reach the end,
                                         Gsus4
            And then I'll start again.
                                  C
            No, I won't leave;
                           F
            I want to try ev-'ry-thing.
                          C               G             C
            I want to try even though I could fail.
                          C                          F
            I won't give up; no, I won't give in
                                   C
            Till I reach the end,
                                         Gsus4
            And then I'll start again.
                                  C
            No, I won't leave;
                           F
            I want to try ev-'ry-thing.
                          C               G             C
            I want to try even though I could fail

            C                F
Interlude   Oh, oh, oh, oh, oh.

            Try ev'rything
            C                Gsus4
            Oh, oh, oh, oh, oh.

            Try ev'rything.
            C                F
            Oh, oh, oh, oh, oh.

            Try ev'rything.
            C       G        C
            Oh, oh, oh, oh, oh.
```

```
Interlude   Look how far you've come;
                                  F
            You filled your heart    with love.
                               C                           G
            Baby, you've done    enough; take a deep breath.
                            C
            Don't beat your-self up;
                            F
            No need to run    so fast.
                            C                    G           C
            Sometimes we come last, but we did our best.


Chorus 2    As Chorus 1

            F           C            Am          G
Bridge      I'll keep on making those new mistakes.
            F           C            Am   G     F
            I'll keep on making them ev'ry    day
                    Am      G       C
            Those new mis - takes.

            C                F
Outro       Oh, oh, oh, oh, oh.

            Try ev'rything.
            C                Gsus4
            Oh, oh, oh, oh, oh.

            Try ev'rything.
            C                F
            Oh, oh, oh, oh, oh.

            Try ev'rything.
            C       G        C
            Oh, oh, oh, oh, oh.
            Am      G          C
            Try ev-'ry-thing.
```

The Unbirthday Song

from ALICE IN WONDERLAND

Words and Music by Mack David,
Al Hoffman and Jerry Livingston

G7#5 C F Dm7 G7 D7 Am7 Adim7

Chorus 1

```
G7#5  C
A     very merry un-birthday to me. To who? To me. Oh, you!
                             Dm7      G7       Dm7     G7
A very merry un-birthday to you. Who, me? Yes, you. Oh, me!
    C                               Dm7
Let's all congratulate us with an-oth-er cup of tea.
  G7                           C     Adim7   G7
A very merry un-birthday to you!
```

Verse 1

```
            C              F                Dm7 G7
Now, sta-tis-tics prove, prove that you've one   birthday.
                                  C
Imagine, just one birthday ev'ry year.
                                   F     C    Dm7  G7
Ah, but there are three hundred and sixty-four  un  -  birthdays.
D7          Am7          D7               G7
Precisely why we're gathered here to cheer.
```

Why then today's my un-birthday too!

It is?

What a small world this is.

In that case...

Chorus 2

```
G7#5  C
A     very merry un-birthday. To me? To you.
                              Dm7 G7 Dm7 G7
A very merry un-birthday. For me?    For  you.
    C                                    Dm7
Now blow the candle out, my dear, and make your wish come true.
  G7                            C    G7    C
A very merry un-birthday  to  you!
```

Un Poco Loco

from COCO

Music by Germaine Franco
Lyrics by Adrian Molina

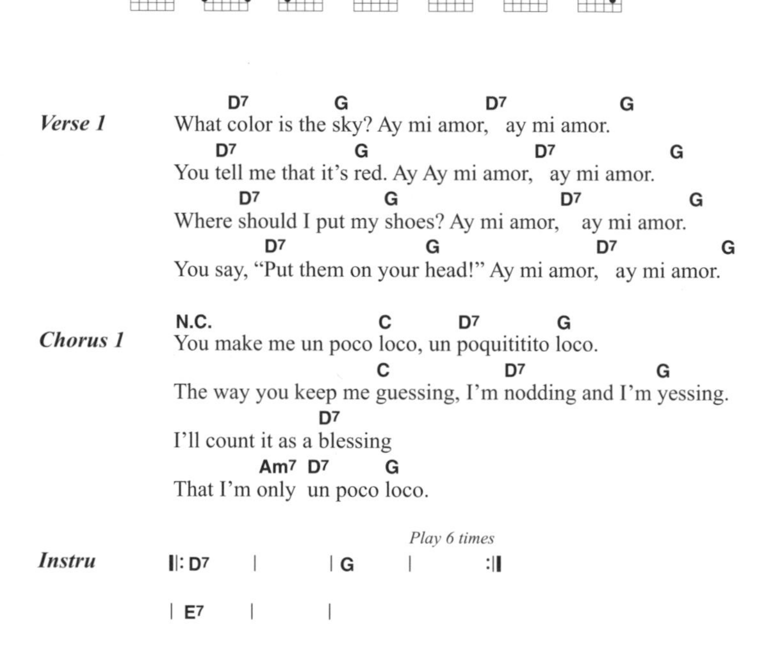

Verse 2

```
A                        D
    The loco that you make    me,
      E7           A
It is just un poco crazy.
                           D
The sense that you're not making,
      E7             A
The liberties you're taking,
                   E7
Leaves my cabeza shaking.
          D   E7        A
You are just un poco loco.
```

Chorus 2

```
                     D            E7          A
He's just un poco crazy, leaves my cabeza shaking.
                     D            E7          A
He's just un poco crazy, leaves my cabeza shaking.
                     D            E7          A
He's just un poco crazy, leaves my cabeza shaking.
                     D            E7          A
He's just un poco crazy, leaves my cabeza shaking.
```

Outro

```
     D              E                    A
Un poquititititititititititititititititito loco.
```

Under the Sea

from THE LITTLE MERMAID

Music by Alan Menken
Lyrics by Howard Ashman

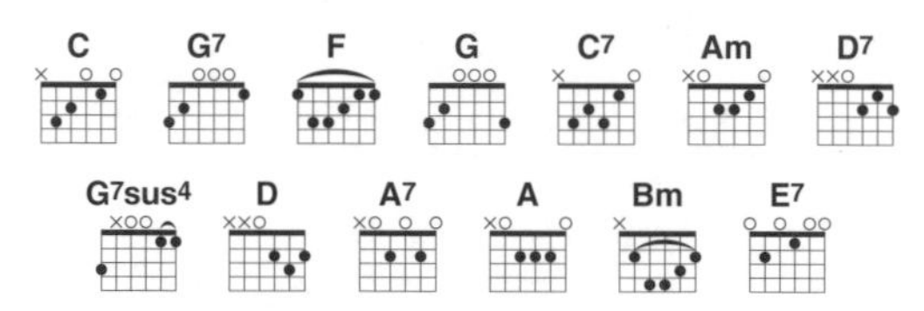

To match original recording, tune guitar down a tone

Verse 1

```
C                         G7         C
    The seaweed is always greener
                       G7      C
    In somebody else's lake.
                            G7      C
    You dream about going up there.
                      G7          C
    But that is a big mis-take.
F                         C
    Just look at the world around you,
G7                            C
    Right here on the ocean floor.
F                            C
    Such wonderful things surround you.
G7                             C
    What more is you lookin' for?
```

```
            N.C          F    C              G7
Chorus 1    Under the sea,     under the sea.
            C                F                          G
              Darlin', it's better down where it's wetter.
                            C
            Take it from me.
            C7               F
              Up on the shore they work all day.
            G                Am
              Out in the sun they slave away.
            D7                  F                      G7                       C   G7 C G7
              While we de-vo-tin' full time to floatin' under the sea.

            C                             G7      C
Verse 2       Down here all the fish is happy
                                           G7          C
              As off through the waves they roll.
                                       G7          C
              The fish on the land ain't happy.
                                          G7    C
              They sad 'cause they in the bowl.
            F                   C
              But fish in the bowl is lucky,
            G7                 C
              They in for a worser fate.
            F                          C
              One day when the boss gets hungry
            G7                           C
              Guess who gon' be on the plate.
```

```
            N.C.        F    C                G7
Chorus 2    Under the sea,    under the sea.
            C           F                       G7        C
               Nobody beat us, fry us and eat us in fricassee.
            C7               F
               We what the land folks love to cook.
            G                Am
               Under the sea we off the hook.
            D7               F                       G7
               We got no troubles, life is the bubbles
                         F    C                G7
            Under the sea.    Under the sea.

            C                F                            G                    G7   C
Verse 3        Since life is sweet here, we got the beat here nat-ur-al-ly.
            C7              F                      G                     Am
               Even the sturgeon an' the ray they get the urge 'n start to play.
            D7              F                      G7                 C
               We got the spirit, you got to hear it under the sea.

            G7  C               G                              C
Bridge               The newt    play the flute. The carp    play the harp.
                          G                              C
            The plaice    play the bass. And they    soundin' sharp.
                        F                              C
            The bass    play the brass. The chub    play the tub.
                         G        G7        C
            The fluke    is the duke of soul.
                       G        G7                C
            The ray    he can play. The lings    on the strings.
                         G        G7        C
            The trout    rockin' out. The blackfish, she sings.
                          F                              C
            The smelt    and the sprat they know    where it's at.
                G        G7         C
            An' oh, that blowfish blow.
```

```
Interlude   | F        | C            | G7        | C        |

            | F        | G7           | C         | C7       |

            | F        | G7           | Am        | D7       |

            | F        | G7sus4  G7   | C         | G7   C   |

            |          | G7      C    | D         | A7   D   |

            |          |              |

                        G    D               A7
Chorus 3    Under the sea,     under the sea.
            D                  G                        A7                     D
               When the sar-dine begin the be-guine it's music to me.
            D7                 G
               What do they got, a lot of sand.
            A              Bm              E7
               We got a hot crustacean band.
                        G                               A7                   D
            Each little clam here know how to jam here under the sea.
            A7   D            G                         A                     D
                    Each little slug here cuttin' a rug here under the sea.
            A7   D           G                                A
                    Each little snail here know how to wail here.
                             Bm                 E7
            That's why it's hotter under the water.
                          G                             A7
            Yeah, we in luck here down in the muck here
                        D    A7  D   A7   D
            Under the sea.
```

We Know the Way

from MOANA

Music by Opetaia Foa'i
Lyrics by Opetaia Foa'i and Lin-Manuel Miranda

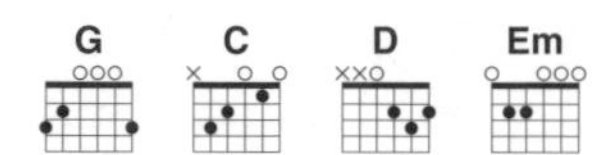

To match original recording, place capo on 2nd fret

Verse 1

```
G
   Tatou tagata folau vala'auina

E le atua o le sami tele e o mai
C                              D
   La ava'e le lu'itau e lelei.
             G
Tapenapena
```

Chorus 1

```
C
   Aue! Aue!
G
Nuku i mua.
D                    G
   Te manulele e ta-ta-ki iei.
C
   Aue! Aue!
G
Te fenua te malie.
D
   Nae ko hakilia kaiga e.
```

Verse 2

```
G
   We read the wind and the sky, when the sun is high.

   We sail the length of the seas on the ocean breeze.
C                                 D
   At night we name ev'ry star;
                        G
We know where we are.

We know who we are, who we are.
```

```
                 C                 G
*Chorus 2*           Away, away,      we set a course to find
                 D                                   G
                     A brand-new island ev-'ry-where we roam.
                 C                     G
                     Away, away, we keep our island in our mind;
                 D
                     And when it's time to find home,

                 We know the way.

                 C                 D
*Chorus 3*           Away, away,
                           Em                          D
                 We are ex-plor-ers reading ev'ry sign.
                 G                           D
                      We tell the stories of our elders
                                     C
                 In a never-ending chain.
                           D
                 Aue! Aue!
                 Em         G
                 Te fenua te malie.
                 D
                     Nae ko hakilia.
                                     G
                 We know the way!
```

We Don't Talk About Bruno

from ENCANTO

Music and Lyrics by Lin-Manuel Miranda

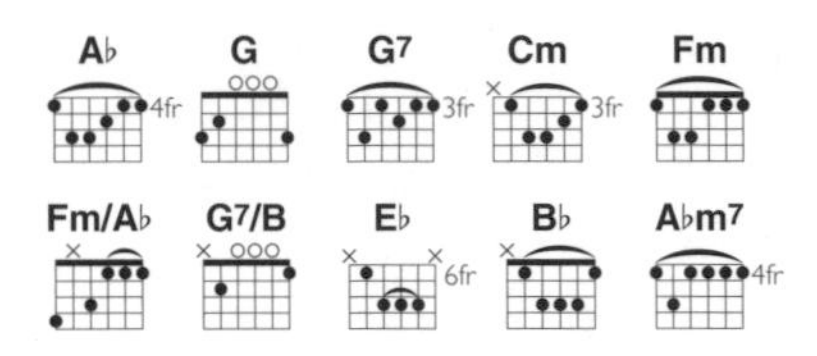

Intro

A♭ G
We don't talk about Bruno, no, no, no!
A♭ G7
We don't talk about Bruno...

Verse 1

Cm Fm
But, it was my wedding day. *(It was our wedding day...)*
G Fm
We were getting ready, and there
Cm Fm
Wasn't a cloud in the sky.
G Fm
(No clouds allowed in the sky)
Cm Fm G Fm
Bruno walks in with a mis-chie-vous grin *(Thunder!!)*
A♭ G7
—You telling this story or am I? *(I'm sorry, mi vida, go on...)*
Cm Fm G Fm
Bruno says, "It looks like rain." *(Why did he tell us?)*
Cm Fm G
In doing so, he floods my brain.
Fm
(Abuela, get the um-brel-las)
Cm Fm G
Married in a hurricane…
Fm
(What a joyous day but anyway…)

Chorus

A♭ G7
We don't talk about Bruno, no, no, no!
A♭ G7
We don't talk about Bruno!

Verse 2

Hey!
Cm Fm
Grew to live in fear of Bruno stuttering or stumbling,
G Fm
I can always hear him sort of muttering and mumbling.
Cm Fm G7
I associate him with the sound of fall-ing sand, ch ch ch
Cm Fm
It's a heavy lift with a gift so humbling,
G Fm
Always left Abuela and the family fumbling,
A♭ G
Grappling with prophecies they couldn't un-der-stand.

Do you understand?
Cm Fm G Fm
A seven-foot frame, rats along his back.
Cm Fm G Fm
When he calls your name it all fades to black.
Cm Fm G Fm
Yeah, he sees your dreams and feasts on your screams.

Chorus

A♭ G7
We don't talk about Bruno, no, no, no!
A♭ G7
We don't talk about Bruno!

Verse 3

```
Cm                    Fm
   He told me my fish would die.
              G7
The next day: dead. (No, no)
Cm                    Fm
   He told me I'd grow a gut!
                  G7
And just like he said... (No, no)
             Cm                       Fm/A♭
He said that all my hair would disappear,
                  G7/B
now look at my head.  (No, no.)
A♭                                        G7
   Your fate is sealed when your prophecy is read!
```

Verse 4

```
E♭                     B♭                                 Cm
He told me that the life of my dreams would be prom - ised,
                 A♭
and someday be mine…
E♭                     B♭
He told me that my power would grow, like the grapes
Cm                                  A♭
    that thrive on the vine…

(Óye, Mariano's on his way)
E♭                     B♭
He told me that the man of my dreams would be just
Cm
    out of reach
A♭
Betrothed to another…
E♭                        B♭
   It's like I hear him now. (Hey, sis)
Cm                                 A♭
   It's like I can hear him now, I can hear him now!
A♭   G
Um, Bruno…
A♭              G
   Yeah, about that Bruno…
```

(*cont.*)

```
Ab                              G
I really need to know a-bout Bruno…
                 Ab                        G
Gimme the truth and the whole truth, Bruno!
     Abm7
```
Is-a-bela, your boyfriend's here.

Time for dinner!

Verse 5

```
Cm               Fm                G                          Fm
   It was my wedding day,     we were getting ready and there
Cm                Fm
Wasn't a cloud     in the sky.
G                             Fm
```
(No clouds allowed   in the sky)
```
Cm                 Fm                G                       Fm
Bruno walks in      with a mis - chie-vous grin     (Thunder!!)
Ab                                        G7
—You telling this story or am I?  (Óye, Mariano's on his...)
Cm                  Fm                   G                  Fm
Bruno says, "It looks like rain."   (Why did he tell us?)
   Cm               Fm                   G
In doing so, he floods my brain.
                              Fm
```
(Abuela, get the um-brel-las...)
```
Cm              Fm           G
Married in a hurricane…
                          Fm
```
(What a joyous day!)
```
Ab                        G7
   Don't talk about Bruno, no!
```
(Why did I talk about Bruno?)
```
Ab                          G7
   Not a word about Bruno!
            G                                      G7     Cm
```
(I never should have brought up Bru-no!)

We Belong Together

from TOY STORY 3

Music and Lyrics by Randy Newman

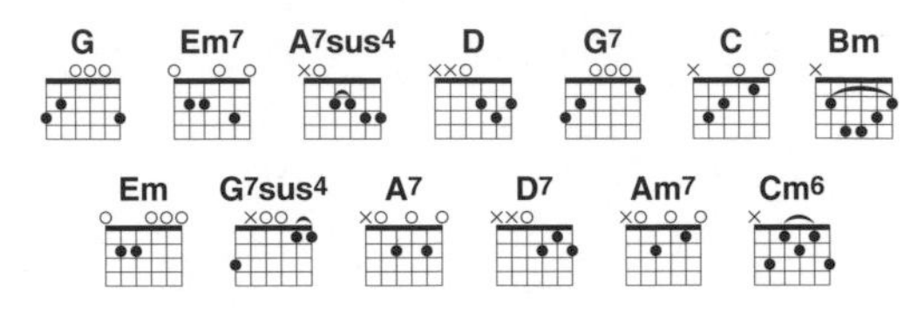

To match original recording, tune guitar down one semitone

Play 6 times

Intro ‖: G Em7 | A7sus4 D :‖

Verse 1

G Em7 A7sus4 D
Don't you turn your back on me;
G Em7 A7sus4 D
Don't you walk away.
G Em7 A7sus4 D
Don't you tell me that I don't care,
G Em7 A7sus4 D
'Cause I do.
G Em7 A7sus4 D
Don't you tell me I'm not the one;
G Em7 A7sus4 D
Don't you tell me I ain't no fun.
G Em7 A7sus4 D G
Just tell me you love me like I love you.
G7 C
You know you do.

```
                         D
cont.         When we're to-geth-er,
              Bm                Em      C
                  Grey skies clear up,
                 D
              And I cheer up
                             G                 G7sus4  G7  C
              To where I'm less depressed.
                     D
              And sin-cere-ly,
                        Bm              Em       A7
              From the bottom of my heart,

              I just can't take it
                              D7    Em7     D7
              When we're a-part.

              G            Em7   C        D
Chorus 1      We   belong    to-geth-er.
                           G7    C
              We   belong    to-geth-er.
                      Cm6   G
              Yes, we do.
                        Em        Am7   D
              You'll be mine for-ev-er
              G            Em7   C      D
              We   belong    to-geth-er.
                           G7    C
              We   belong    to-geth-er.
                              Cm6   G
              You know it's true.
                                         Em      Am7   D
              It's gonna stay this way    for-ev-er,    me and you.


Interlude     | G          Em7     | A7sus4    D        |

              | G          Em7     | A7sus4    D        |
```

Verse 2

```
G     Em7             A7sus4     D
    If I could really talk to you,
G                Em7  A7sus4  D
    If I could find a way,
G              Em7             A7sus4       D            G
    I'm not shy, there's a whole lot I        wanna say.
Em7           A7sus4          D
   Of course         there is.
G              Em7              A7sus4    D
Talk about friendship and loyalty,
G              Em7               A7sus4      D
Talk about how much you mean to me,
G              Em7          A7sus4     D         G
   And I'd promise to always be by your side
      G7                         C
When-ev-er you'd need me.
            D
The day I met you
        Bm                    Em     C
Was the luckiest day of my life,
      D              G
And I bet you feel the same,
        G7sus4        G7    C
'Least I hope you do.
                 D
So don't forget    me
      Bm                            Em    A7
If the future should take you a-way.

You know you'll always be
D7      Em7    D7
Part of me.
```

```
                G              Em7   C        D
*Chorus 2*      We   belong    to-geth-er.
                              G7    C
                We   belong    to-geth-er.
                             Cm6
                'Way that I see it,
                G                     Em       Am7    D
                  It's gon' be this way for-ev-er.
                G              Em7   C        D
                We   belong    to-geth-er.
                              G7    C
                We   belong    to-geth-er.
                     Cm6    G              Em              Am7   D
                Honestly.        We'll go on    this way for-ev-er.
                            G  Em7  A7sus4  D  G  Em7  A7sus4  D
                You and me.
                            G  Em7  A7sus4  D  G  Em7  A7sus4  D
                You and me.

                                                  Repeat to fade
Outro           ||: G          Em7      | A7sus4      D         :||
```

We're All in This Together

from HIGH SCHOOL MUSICAL

Words and Music by Matthew Gerrard and Robbie Nevil

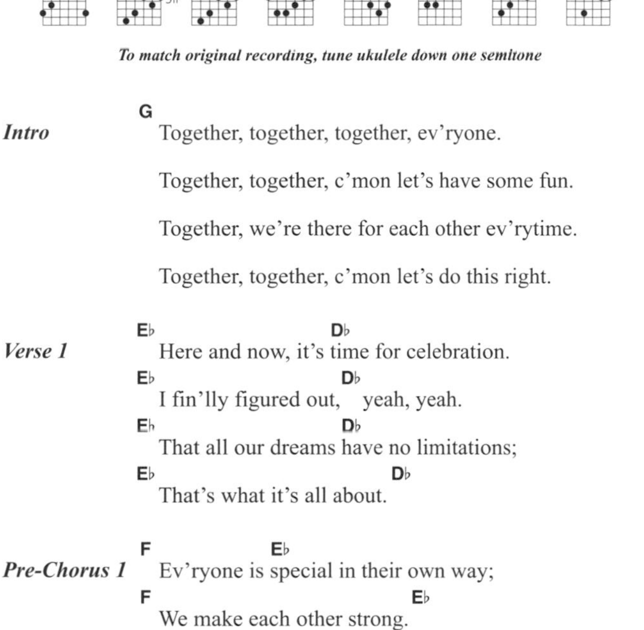

To match original recording, tune ukulele down one semitone

Intro

G
Together, together, together, ev'ryone.

Together, together, c'mon let's have some fun.

Together, we're there for each other ev'rytime.

Together, together, c'mon let's do this right.

Verse 1

E♭ D♭
Here and now, it's time for celebration.
E♭ D♭
I fin'lly figured out, yeah, yeah.
E♭ D♭
That all our dreams have no limitations;
E♭ D♭
That's what it's all about.

Pre-Chorus 1

F E♭
Ev'ryone is special in their own way;
F E♭
We make each other strong.
F E♭
We're not the same; we're diff'rent in a good way.
F E♭ F
Together's where we belong.

```
               G          D     Em
Chorus 1       We're all in this  to-geth-er;
               G              C
               Once we know  that we are,
               G               C               D
                We're all stars,  and we see  that.
                   G          D     Em
               We're all in this  to-geth-er,
               G            C                   G
               And it shows  when we stand  hand in hand,
               C                         D                Fsus2
                 Make our dreams  come true.

               Ev'rybody now:


Interlude      As Intro

               Eb                       Db
Verse 2           We're all here, and speaking out with one voice.
               Eb                                   Db
                  We're gonna rock the house,     yeah, yeah.
               Eb                           Db
                  The party's on; now ev'rybody make some noise.
               Eb                                      Db
                  Come on and scream and shout.

               F                       Eb
Pre-Chorus 2      We've arrived be-cause we stuck together,
               F                             Eb    F
                  Champions one and all.
```

Chorus 2

```
         G          D    Em
We're all in this    to-geth-er;
G                C
Once we know   that we are,
G                  C              D
  We're all stars,   and we see    that.
         G          D    Em
We're all in this    to-geth-er,
G               C                G
And it shows    when we stand    hand in hand,
C                         D
   Make our dreams    come true.
         G          D    Em
We're all in this    to-geth-er;
G                  C
When we reach     we can fly,
G                  C               D
    Know inside    we can make    it.
         G          D    Em
We're all in this    to-geth-er,
G              C                     G
Once we see    there's a chance
               C              D
That we have    and we take    it.
```

Outro

```
Fsus2
Wildcats ev'rywhere,

Wave your hands up in the air.

That's the way we do it;

Let's get to it,
                     G
C'mon, ev'ryone!
```

When She Loved Me

from TOY STORY 2

Music and Lyrics by Randy Newman

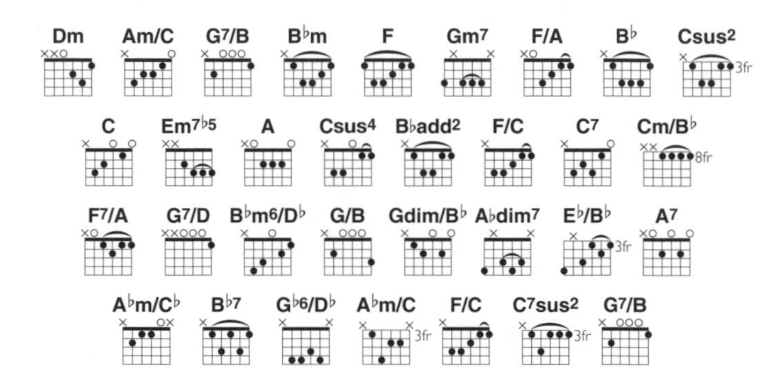

Intro | Dm Am/C | G7/B B♭m | F | |

Chorus 1

Gm7 F/A
When some-body loved me,
B♭ G7/B C
Ev-'ry-thing was beautiful.
Em7♭5 A Dm Csus4
Ev'ry hour we spent to-geth-er
B♭add2 C
Lives within my heart.
F Gm7 F/A
And when she was sad,
B♭ G7/B Csus2 C
I was there to dry her tears;
Em7♭5 A Dm Csus4 B♭add2
And when she was happy, so was I,
F/C C7 F
When she loved me.

```
           B♭
*Verse 1*  Through the summer and the fall,
              F/C        Cm/B♭ F7/A     B♭
           We had each other,  that was all.
               F/C      B♭   F/C     G7/D
           Just she and I to-geth-er,
           G7/B                          C
           Like it was meant to be.
           F           Gm7    F/A
           And when she was lonely,
           B♭    G7/B    C
           I was there to comfort her,
                  F7/A  B♭  F/C  C7    F
           And I knew that she  loved me.

           Dm                     B♭m6/D♭
*Verse 2*  So the years went by;
                          F/C
           I stayed the same.
              G/B     Gdim/B♭ F/A      Fm6/A♭
           But she be-gan  to   drift  a-way;
           E♭/B♭  A7   Dm
           I was left a-lone.
           B♭m6/D♭  C7       A♭m/C♭ B♭7
           Still   I   waited for the  day when she'd say,
            G♭6/D♭          A♭m/C♭  C7
           "I will always love      you."
```

Verse 3

```
F          Gm7     F/A
Lonely and for-got-ten,
B♭      G7/B           C
Never thought she'd look my way,
Em7♭5                  A          Dm       Fadd2/C
And she smiled at me and held me
     B♭add2             C
Just like she used to do,
          F7/A  B♭
Like she loved me
             F/C   C
When she loved me.
```

Chorus 2

```
F              Gm7  F/A
When some-body loved me,
B♭      G7/B      C
Ev-'ry-thing was beautiful.
Em7♭5 A         Dm        Csus4
Ev'ry  hour we spent to-geth-er
B♭add2            C
Lives within my heart.
        F/C  C7     F
When she  loved  me.
```

A Whole New World

from ALADDIN

Music by Alan Menken
Lyrics by Tim Rice

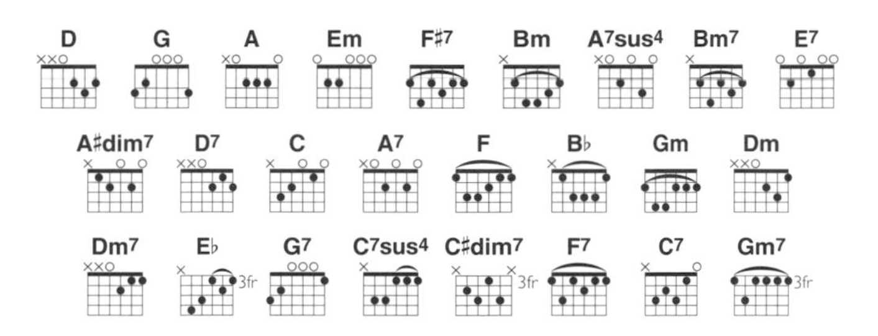

Verse 1

D
I can show you the world,
G A
Shining, shimmering, splen-did.
Em F♯7 Bm
Tell me, princess, now when did
G D A7sus4
You last let your heart de-cide?
D
I can open your eyes,
G A
Take you wonder by won-der,
Em F♯7 Bm
Over, sideways and under
G D
On a magic carpet ride.

Chorus 1

                    A   D
A whole new world,
                 A   D
A new fan-tas-tic point of view.
                 G   D
No one to tell us no
     G   D
Or where to go
     Bm7   E7   A7sus4
Or say we're only   dreaming.
                    A   D
A whole new world,
                 A   A♯dim7   Bm
A dazzling place I never   knew.
D7   G   D
But when I'm way up here,
     G   D
It's crystal clear
         Bm7   E7   C   A7   D
That now I'm in a whole new world with you.

Verse 2

F
Unbelievable sights,
                       B♭   C
Indescribable feel-ing.
Gm   A7   Dm
Soaring, tumbling, free-wheeling
                  B♭   F
Through an endless diamond sky.

```
                          C          F
Chorus 2     A whole new world,
                        C                              F
             A hundred thousand things to see.
                      B♭                 F
             I'm like a shooting star,
                 B♭               F
             I've come so far;
               Dm7      G7         C7sus4
             I can't go back to where I used to be.
                          C         F
             A whole new world,
                          C          C♯dim7         Dm
             With new ho-ri-zons to          pursue
             F7                    B♭    F
             I'll chase them an-y-where.
                       B♭        F
             There's time to spare.
             Dm7    G7           E♭              C7              Dm      F
             Let me share this whole new world with you.

                          B♭        F
Outro        A whole new world,
                                    Gm7
             That's where we'll be.
             F                 B♭
                A thrilling chase,
                            C7sus4                F
             A wondrous place for you and me.
```

When Will My Life Begin?

from TANGLED

Music by Alan Menken
Lyrics by Glenn Slater

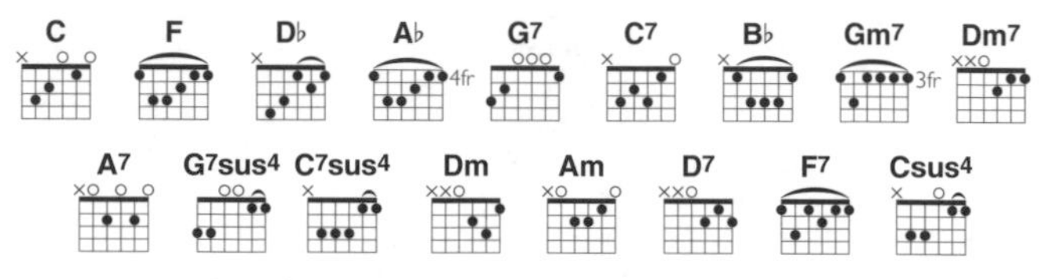

To match original recording, tune guitar down one semitone

Verse 1

C F
Seven a.m., the usual morning line up.
C F
Start on the chores, and sweep 'til the floor's all clean.
D♭ A♭
Polish and wax, do laundry, and mop, and shine up.
C F G7 C7
Sweep a-gain, and by then it's, like, seven fif-teen.
F B♭ Gm7 F
And so I'll read a book, or maybe two or three;
Dm7 G7 B♭ F
I'll add a few more paintings to my gal-le-ry;
Dm7 G7
I'll play gui-tar, and knit,
B♭ A7 Dm7
And cook, and ba - sic -'ly just wonder,
G7sus4 C7sus4 F C7 F C7 F
"When will my life be-gin?"

Verse 2

C F
Then after lunch, it's puzzles, and darts and baking…
C F
Papier mâché, a bit of ballet and chess…
D♭ A♭
Pottery and ventriloquy, can-dle-mak-ing…
C F G7 C7
Then I'll stretch, maybe sketch, take a climb, sew a dress.
F B♭ Gm7 F
And I'll re-read the books if I have time to spare.
Dm7 G7
I'll paint the walls some more;
B♭ F
I'm sure there's room some-where.
Dm7 G7
And then I'll brush and brush
B♭ A7 Dm7
And brush, and brush my hair,
G7sus4 B♭ A Dm
Stuck in the same place I've al - ways been,
G7sus4 F
And I'll keep wond'ring and wond'ring
B♭ Am D7
And wond'ring and wond -'ring,
G7sus4 C7sus4 F
"When will my life be-gin?"

Outro

F B♭
Tomorrow night…
F B♭
The lights will ap-pear,
F B♭ F Gm7 C
Just like they do on my birthday each year.
Dm7 G7 C7sus4 F7
What is it like out there where they glow?
B♭ F
Now that I'm older,
B♭ Csus4 C
Mother might just let me go…

Winnie the Pooh

from THE MANY ADVENTURES OF WINNIE THE POOH*

Words and Music by Richard M. Sherman
and Robert B. Sherman

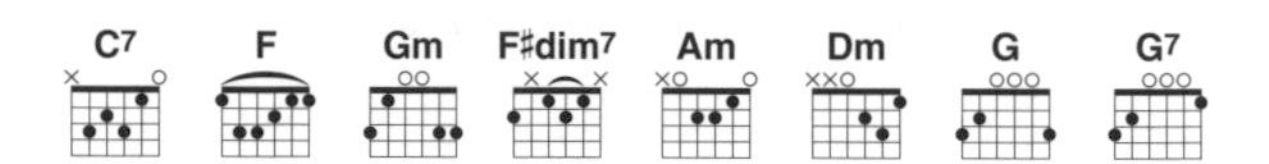

Verse 1

Gm C7 F F♯dim7
Deep in the hundred acre wood
Gm C7 Fmaj7
Where Christopher Robin plays,
F♯dim7 Gm C7 Am Dm
You'll find the en-chant-ed neighbor-hood
G7 C7 F
Of Christopher's childhood days.

Verse 2

Gm C7 F F♯dim7
A donkey named Eeyore is his friend,
Gm C7 F
And Kanga and Little Roo.
Gm C7 F Dm
There's Rabbit and Piglet and there's Owl,
G7 C7 F
But most of all, Winnie the Pooh.

*Based on the "Winnie the Pooh" works, by A. A. Milne and E. H. Shepard

Chorus 1

C7
Winnie the Pooh,
F
Winnie the Pooh.
C7
Tubby, little cubby
    F
All stuffed with fluff.
     C7
He's Winnie the Pooh,
F
Winnie the Pooh.
C7   F
Willy nilly silly old bear.

Outro

C7   F   C7   F
Willy nilly silly old bear.

The World Es Mi Familia

from COCO

Music by Germaine Franco
Lyrics by Adrian Molina

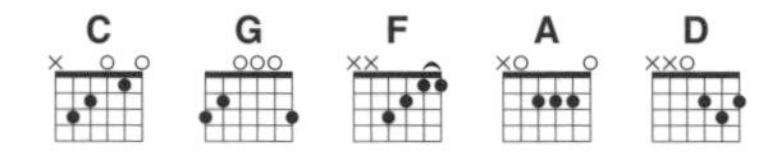

Verse

C
Se-ño-ras y señores,
G
Buenas tardes, buenas noches.

Buenas tardes, buenas noches,
C
Señoritas y se-ño-res,

To be here with you tonight
G
Brings me joy! ¡Qué a-le-gría!

For this music is my language
C F C
And the world es mi fa-mi-lia.

Chorus

G C
For this music is my language
F C
And the world es mi fa-mi-lia.
G C
For this music is my language
F C A
And the world es mi fa-mi-lia.
D
For this music is my langua–, ah!

You'll Be in My Heart
(Pop Version)
from TARZAN®

Words and Music by Phil Collins

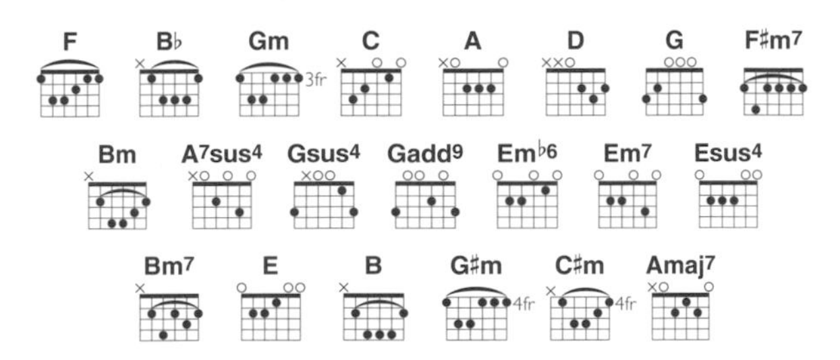

To match original recording, place capo on 1st fret

Intro

F
Come stop your crying, it will be all right.

Just take my hand, hold it tight.

B♭
I will protect you from all around you.

Gm   C
I will be here, don't you   cry.

Verse 1

F   C   F
For one so small you seem so strong.

                                                  C   F
My arms will hold you, keep you safe and warm.

B♭
This bond between us can't be broken.

Gm   C
I will be here, don't you   cry.

Chorus 1

```
A        D              G
   'Cause you'll be in my heart,
     A                F#m7      Bm
Yes, you'll be in my heart from this day on
     G               C     A
Now   and for-ev-er-more.
D                G        A                F#m7
You'll be in my heart no matter what they say.
        Bm        G         C     A7sus4  G   A
You'll be in my heart al-ways.
```

Verse 1

```
F                                   C       F
   Why can't they understand the way we feel?
                                C      F
They just don't trust what they can't ex-plain.
Bb
   I know we're diff'rent, but deep inside us
Gm                         C
   We're not that diff'rent at all.
```

Chorus 2

```
A      D             G
   And you'll be in my heart,
     A                F#m7      Bm
Yes, you'll be in my heart from this day on
     G               C
Now   and for-ev-er-more.
```

Bridge

Gsus4 G Gadd9 G
Don't listen to them, 'cause what do they know?

(What do they know?)
Em♭6 Em7 Esus4 Em7
We need each other to have, to hold.
Bm7 C
They'll see in time, I know.
Gsus4 G Gadd9 G
When destiny calls you, you must be strong.

(Gotta be strong.)
Em♭6 Em7 Esus4 Em7
I may not be with you, but you've got to hold on.
Bm7 C
They'll see in time, I know.
D A
We'll show them to-geth-er, 'cause

Chorus 3

E A
You'll be in my heart,
B G♯m
Believe me you'll be in my heart.
C♯m A D B
I'll be there from this day on, now and for-ev-er-more.
E A
You'll be in my heart
B G♯m
(You'll be here in my heart.) No matter what they say.
C♯m A
(I'll be with you.) You'll be here in my heart
D
(I'll be there.) al-ways.
B Amaj7 E
Al-ways I'll be with you.
Amaj7 E
I'll be there for you always, always and al - ways.
Amaj7 E
Just look over your shoulder. Just look over your shoulder.
Amaj7 E
Just look over your shoulder, I'll be there always.

Yo Ho

(A Pirate's Life for Me)

from Disney Parks' 'Pirates of the Caribbean' Attraction

Words by Xavier Atencio
Music by George Bruns

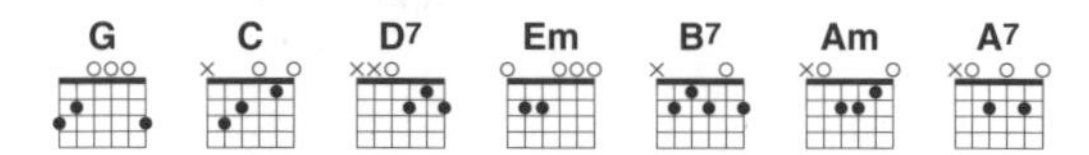

To match original recording, tune guitar down one tone

Verse 1

```
G       C G                D7      G
Yo ho, yo ho, a pirate's life for me.
    Em                        B7
We pillage, plunder, we rifle and loot.
       Em                     B7
Drink up me 'earties, yo ho.
    Am           D7           G            Em
We kidnap and ravage and don't give a hoot.
       A7                     D7
Drink up me 'earties, yo ho.
```

Verse 2

```
G       C G                D7      G
Yo ho, yo ho, a pirate's life for me.
    Em                        B7
We extort and pilfer, we filch and sack.
       Em                     B7
Drink up me 'earties, yo ho.
     Am            D7           G        Em
Ma-raud and em-bezzle and even hi-jack.
       A7                     D7
Drink up me 'earties, yo ho.
```

Verse 3

G C G D7 G
Yo ho, yo ho, a pirate's life for me.
Em B7
We kindle and char and in-flame and ignite.
Em B7
Drink up me 'earties, yo ho.
Am D7 G Em
We burn up the city, we're really a fright.
A7 D7
Drink up me 'earties, yo ho.

Outro

B7 Em B7
We're rascals and scoundrels, we're villains and knaves.
Em B7
Drink up me 'earties, yo ho.
Am D7 G Em
We're devils and black sheep, we're really bad eggs.
A7 D7
Drink up me 'earties, yo ho.
G C G D7 G
Yo ho, yo ho, a pirate's life for me.

You Can Fly! You Can Fly! You Can Fly!

from PETER PAN

Words by Sammy Cahn
Music by Sammy Fain

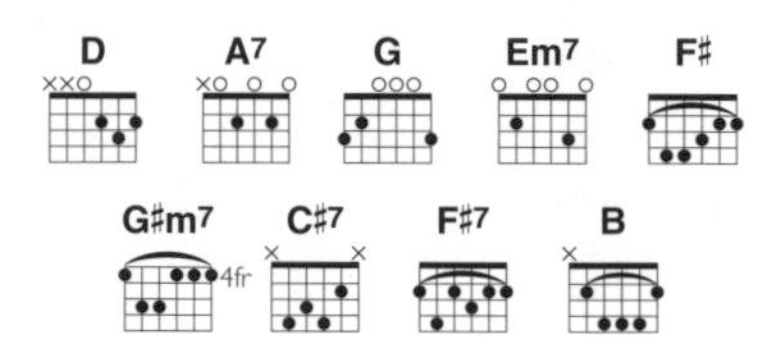

To match original recording, place capo on 1st fret

```
             D
*Verse 1*    Think of a wonderful thought,

             Any merry little thought.
             A7                    D
             Think of Christmas, think of snow,
             A7                    D
             Think of sleigh bells, off you go!
                  G
             Like reindeer in the sky.
             A7       D              Em7  A7       D
             You can fly! You can fly!    You can fly!


*Verse 2*    Think of the happiest things,

             It's the same as having wings.
             A7                D
             Take the path that moonbeams make.
             A7                  D
             If the moon is still a-wake.
                     G
             You'll see him wink his eye.
             A7       D              Em7  A7       D
             You can fly! You can fly!    You can fly!
```

Bridge

F♯ G♯m7 C♯7
Up you go with a heigh and ho,
F♯ G♯m7 C♯7
To the stars be-yond the blue.
F♯ F♯7 B
There's a Never Land waiting for you
F♯ G♯m7 C♯7 F♯
Where all your happy dreams come true.
Em7 A7 D
Every dream that you dream will come true.

Verse 3

D
When there's a smile in your heart

There's no better time to start.
A7 D
Think of all the joy you'll find
A7 D
When you leave the world behind
G
And bid your cares goodbye.
A7 D A7 D Em7 D Em7 D
You can fly! You can fly! You can fly!

You're Welcome

from MOANA

Music and Lyrics by Lin-Manuel Miranda

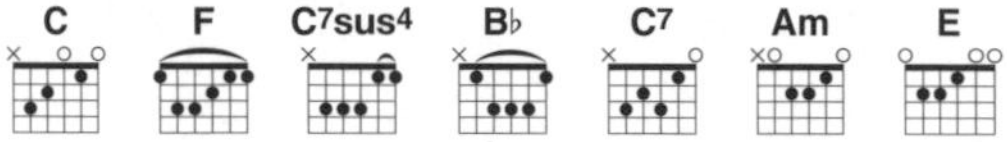

C F C7sus4 B♭ C7 Am E

Verse 1

C F
I see what's happening, yeah:
C7sus4 C
You're face to face with greatness, and it's strange.
F
You don't even know how you feel, it's a-do-ra-ble.
C7sus4 C
Well, it's nice to see that humans never change.
F
Open your eyes, let's be-gin:
C7sus4
Yes, it's really me, it's Maui, breathe it in,
C F
I know it's a lot: the hair, the bod,
B♭ C7
When you're staring at a demigod.

Chorus 1

Am F C
What can I say except, "You're wel - come,
E Am
For the tides, the sun, the sky"?
F C
Hey, it's okay, it's okay: you're wel - come.
E C
I'm just an ordinary demiguy.

Verse 2

F
Hey, what has two thumbs and pulled up the sky
C7sus4
When you were waddling yea high? This guy!
C
When the nights got cold,
F
Who stole you fire from down below?
C7sus4
You're looking at him, yo.
C F
Oh, also, I lassoed the sun.

You're welcome.
C7sus4 C
To stretch your days and bring you fun.
F
Also, I harnessed the breeze.

You're welcome.
B♭ C7 Am
To fill your sails and shake your trees.

Chorus 2

Am F C
So what can I say except, "You're wel - come,
E Am
For the is - lands I pulled from the sea"?
F C
There's no need to pray, it's okay, you're wel - come.
E Am
Huh! I guess it's just my way of being me!
F C
You're wel - come! You're wel - come!
C5
Well, come to think of it:

Rap

C N.C.
Kid, honestly, I could go on and on.

I could explain ev'ry nat'ral phenomenon.
C N.C.
The tide? The grass? The ground?

Oh, that was Maui, just messing around.
C N.C.
I killed an eel, I buried its guts,

Sprouted a tree: now you got coconuts!
C N.C.
What's the lesson? What is the takeaway?

Don't mess with Maui when he's on a breakaway.
Am N.C.
And the tapestry here in my skin
F N.C.
Is a map of the vict'ries I win!
C N.C.
Look where I've been! I make ev'rything happen!
E
Look at that mean mini Maui, just tickety

Tappin'! Heh, heh, heh,

Heh, heh, heh, hey!

Outro

```
Am                  F                       C
        Well, anyway,  let me say, "You're wel - come,
            E                          Am
For the won - derful world you know."
              F                      C
Hey, it's okay,   it's okay: you're wel - come.
      E                              Am
Well, come to think of it, I gotta go.
                 F                      C
Hey, it's your day   to say, "You're wel - come,"
       E                            Am
'Cause I'm gonna need that boat.
                 F                      C
I'm sailing away,   away. You're wel - come,
       E                                Am
'Cause Maui can do ev'rything but float!
            F                      C
You're wel - come! You're wel - come!
F   C  N.C.                   C
       And thank you!
```

You've Got a Friend in Me

from TOY STORY

Music and Lyrics by Randy Newman

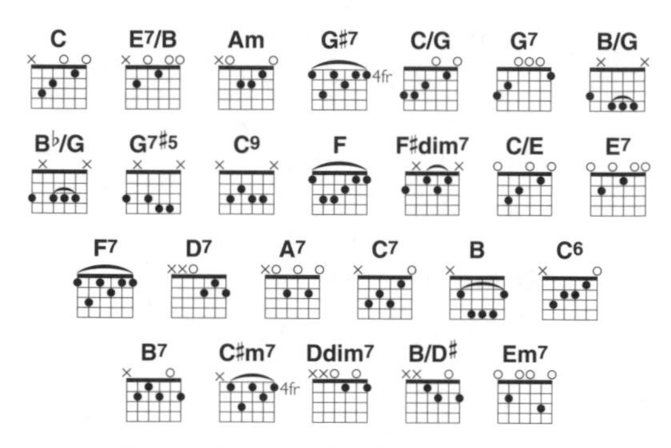

To match original recording, place capo on 3rd fret

Intro

| C E7/B | Am G♯7 | C/G G7 |

| C B/G | B♭/G B/G |

Verse 1

C G7♯5 C C9
You've got a friend in me.
F F♯dim7 C/G C
You've got a friend in me.
F C/E E7 Am
When the road looks rough ahead
F C/E E7 Am
And you're miles and miles from your nice warm bed,
F F♯dim7 C/G C F7 E7 Am
You just re-mem-ber what your old pal said:
D7 G7 C A7
Son, you got a friend in me.
D7 G7
Yeah, you've got a friend in me.

Instru

| C E7/B | Am G♯7 | C/G G7 |

Verse 2

C G7♯5 C C9
You've got a friend in me.
F F♯dim7 C/G C
You've got a friend in me.
F C/E E7 Am
You got troubles, then I got 'em, too.
F C/E E7 Am
There isn't anything I wouldn't do for you.
F F♯dim7 C/G C F7 E7 Am
If we stick to-geth-er we can see it through,
D7 G7 C A7
'Cause you've got a friend in me.
D7 G7 C7
Yeah, you've got a friend in me.

Bridge

F B
Now, some other folks might be a little bit smarter than I am,
C6 B7 C6
Bigger and stronger, too, maybe.
B C♯m7 Ddim7 B/D♯ Em7 A7
But none of them will ever love you the way I do,
Dm7 G7
Just me and you, boy.

Verse 3

C G7♯5 C C9
And as the years go by,
F F♯dim7 C/G C
Our friendship will never die.
F F♯dim7 C E7 Am
You're gonna see it's our des - ti - ny.
D7 G7 C A7
You've got a friend in me.
D7 G7 C A7
You've got a friend in me.
D7 G7 C E7/B
You've got a friend in me.

Outro

| Am G♯7 | C/G G7 | C |

Zero to Hero

from HERCULES

Music by Alan Menken
Lyrics by David Zippel

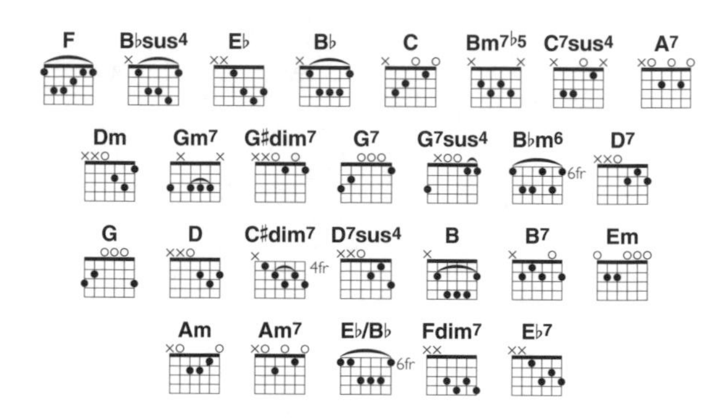

Intro | F | B♭sus4 | F | B♭sus4 |

Verse 1

```
F                E♭              F
Bless my soul, Herc was on a roll,
E♭              F                B♭                  C
Person of the week in ev'ry Greek opinion poll.
F              E♭                 F
What a pro, Herc could stop a show.
E♭              F                      B♭          Bm7♭5
Point him at a monster and you're talkin' S.R.O.
C7sus4                E♭  F  E♭  F
He was a no one, a ze - ro, ze - ro.
C7sus4                E♭  F  E♭  F
Now he's a honcho, he's a he - ro.
C7sus4                    A7        Dm
Here was a kid with his act down pat.
      Gm7  F    B♭   Bm7♭5  B♭      F
From zero  to   hero        in no time flat.
Gm7  F    B♭  Bm7♭5 B♭       F
Zero to   hero,         just like that.
```

```
             B♭                          C
Verse 2      When he smiled the girls   went wild
                       F          Gm7          G♯dim7    F
             With       oohs       and ahs.
                        B♭                         C
             And they slapped his face  on   ev'ry vase.
                  F  Gm7     G♯dim7    F
             On      ev'ry    vase.
                         A7                       Dm
             From ap-pear-ance fees and royalties,
                  A7                          Dm
             Our Herc had cash to burn.
                    G7          G7sus4    B♭m6
             Now nouveau riche and famous
             G7          C7sus4                            D7
             He could tell you what's a Grecian urn.

             G           F                G
Verse 3      Say amen, there he goes a-gain.
             F                  G                  C                         D/F♯
             Sweet and un-de-feat-ed and an awesome ten for ten.
             G                 F                   G
             Folks lined up  just to watch him flex,
             F                    G                     C                  C♯dim7
             And this perfect package packed a pair of perfect pecs.
             D7sus4                           G
             Hercie, he comes, he sees,    he conquers.
             D7sus4                       G
             Honey, the crowds were going bonkers.
             D7sus4                    B       B7   Em
             He showed the moxie, brains and spunk,
                     Am   G    C      A7     C      G
             From zero  to    hero,       a major hunk.
             Am7  G   C     A7       D7sus4
             Zero  to   hero     and who'd a-thunk?
```

Interlude | G C | G C G | C | G C G |

Verse 4

C G C G C G
Who put the glad in glad-i-a-tor? Her-cu-les.
C G C G C G
Whose daring deeds are great the-a-ter? Her-cu-les.
B♭ E♭ B♭ E♭ B♭
Is he bold? No one brav-er.
D7 C Fdim7 D7
Is he sweet? Our fav'rite flavor.

Verse 5

G G7 C D7sus4
Her-cu-les.
G G7 C D7sus4
Her-cu-les.
G G7 C D7sus4
Her-cu-les.
G G7 C D7sus4
Her-cu-les.
G G7 C D7sus4
Her-cu-les.
G G7 C D7sus4
Her-cu-les.
G G C D7♯
Bless my soul, Herc was on a roll, undefeated.
G C E♭7
Riding high, and the nicest guy. Not con-cei-ted.
D7sus4 F G F G
He was a nothing, ze - ro, ze - ro.
D7sus4 F G F G
Now he's a honcho, he's a he - ro.
D7sus4 B7 Em
He hit the heights at break-neck speed.
Am7 G C C♯dim7 C Am7 G C C♯dim7 C
From zero to he - ro. Herc is a he-ro.
Am7 G C C♯dim7 C D7sus4 D G7
Now he's a he-ro. Yes, indeed.